AF413304

THE MOST INSPIRATIONAL BASEBALL STORIES FOR YOUNG READERS

15
AMAZING & INSPIRING
TRUE TALES

FROM MODERN BASEBALL GREATS

TERRENCE ARMSTRONG

Copyright © 2024 Terrence Armstrong
All rights reserved.

This book's content may not be reproduced, duplicated, or transmitted without explicit written permission from the author or publisher.

Under no circumstances shall the publisher, author, or anyone else be held responsible for any blame, legal liability, damages, reparation, or monetary loss arising from the information in this book, either directly or indirectly.

Legal Notice:

This book is protected by copyright and is intended for personal use only. Any alteration, distribution, sale, use, quotation, or paraphrasing of any part or content within this book requires the consent of the author or publisher.

Disclaimer Notice:

The information in this document is provided for educational and entertainment purposes only. Every effort has been made to present accurate, up-to-date, reliable, and complete information, but no warranties of any kind are declared or implied. Readers should be aware that the author is not providing legal, financial, medical, or professional advice.

By reading this document, the reader agrees that the author is not responsible under any circumstances for any direct or indirect losses resulting from the use of the information contained within, including, but not limited to, errors, omissions, or inaccuracies.

CONTENTS

INTRODUCTION
STRIVING FOR GREATNESS

Have you ever wanted to be great? Has there ever been anything that you were so passionate about, that nothing but greatness would do? The baseball players mentioned in this book all had goals that they worked hard to achieve. Mark McGwire knocking balls out of the park or Nolan Ryan pitching no hitters—all of these players always gave it their all.

Some players such as Ken Griffey Jr. felt they had a lot to live up to. Ken's dad after all was a great baseball player in his own right. Ken Griffey Jr. had some pretty big shoes to fill, but he didn't let that bother him—he just put his time in at the batting cage just like everyone else. He perfected his game and learned a lot of valuable life lessons along the way.

So too, did Derek Jeter. Derek played shortstop for the Yankees and learned to become a real team player. He was literally right in the middle of the action, making sure the ball got where it needed to be. He learned that no matter what position you're given in life—whether it's shortstop or something else entirely—you should make the best of it.

All of the life lessons learned by these greats are readily applicable to our own lives today. This book follows the paths that these baseball greats took and what they learned along the way.

Twins

HOW DAVID ORTIZ BECAME BASEBALL'S BIG PAPI

David Ortiz captured the world's attention in 2008 when he led the Boston Red Sox to victory over the Tampa Bay Rays. It was a do-or-die moment for the Red Sox, since losing to Tampa would have meant the end of their season and missing out on the World Series. The Red Sox weren't doing so great, however, and by the seventh inning, victory seemed almost certain for the Tampa Bay Rays. That is, until beloved heavy hitter David Ortiz stepped up to the plate.

With fans going wild and screaming for their "Big Papi," the six-foot four slugger steadied his bat and waited for the pitch. The pitcher from the Tampa Bay Rays, Grant Balfour, hurled the baseball toward David, and the next thing anyone knew, his bat erupted in a thunderous crack as the baseball went soaring high into the air.

The ball was launched well out of reach of Tampa Bay's outfielders. David Ortiz had hit a home run. Since the ball had been knocked so far from the field, any players on base were free to run to home plate to score points for their team. And this is precisely what happened.

David's Red Sox teammates Coco Crisp and Dustin Pedroia were already on base, and were able to run home. David Ortiz, himself, was also able to run all the way to home plate. This changed the trajectory of the whole game, and the Red Sox ended up the big winners.

But what about the one they call the Big Papi? How did he get to this point?

Life for the baseball star known as Big Papi began on November 18th, 1975, when he was born in the Dominican Republic. The Dominican Republic is located on an island in the Caribbean, hundreds of miles away from the US mainland.

That's a fairly long distance, but the American love of baseball is not far away. Baseball is popular in the region, and many breakout stars who later emerged in the MLB have hailed from there. David grew up loving the sport and found any excuse he could to play it.

He soon became known for his great athletic ability—especially his ability to hit home runs. It was this ability that got the attention of scouts for the Seattle Mariners, who ended up recruiting David as a teenager in the early 1990s. He then left the Mariners for the Minnesota Twins in 1997. He was a standout player for the Twins that year, and developed a reputation as a heavy hitter.

The 1999 season saw David's ability begin to slip. Twins management was disappointed with the less-than-stellar performance, and decided to let David go. He ended up playing for a much more obscure team in the Minor League called the "Salt Lake Stingers." This was a disappointing development. David had been on the fast track to success, only to be demoted.

David might have been tempted to give up at this point, but he persevered. He knew deep down that he couldn't quit. He had worked so hard to make something of himself, and he couldn't give up now. Instead of giving up, he redoubled his efforts and managed to convince the Minnesota Twins to bring him back for the 2000 season.

He was back in the Majors, but the Twins still struggled to come out on top. In fact, they seemed to lose more than they won. Since baseball is a team effort, this wasn't all David's fault. There were many reasons why the Twins were a little less than successful. Nevertheless, David did his part to help when he could.

David always did his best, both on and off the field, to make the best of any given situation. Even when the team was doing poorly, David kept a positive, upbeat attitude. In fact, he became known for his smile and good-natured demeanor. Even when things were not going so well during the course of a game, he was known to give words of encouragement to his teammates.

In 2001, however, David himself was the one in need of encouragement, and it had nothing at all to do with baseball. His mother died in a tragic car crash. She meant the world to him, and he was very sad to hear the news. It took some time for him to get over his sadness, but tapping into his own inner strength, he came out of this period of mourning stronger than ever.

David would later remark about how his mother's passing seemed to put things into perspective for him. He no longer stressed out as much about his performance, nor did he obsess about baseball as much as he had in the past. As much as he loved the game, his mom's passing made him realize that it was indeed just a game. He would do his best, but he wouldn't let it get to him if things didn't work out.

David had a renewed sense of confidence and purpose, and his 2002 run with the Twins was much improved. He was now hitting more home runs (20 that season), and the outlook for the Twins was much better. Unfortunately, David was also getting injured and having periodic batting slumps as a result of his injuries.

As good as he was, David had become a bit of an unpredictable wild card. By the time the 2003 season rolled around, both the management of the Twins and David himself were looking for a change. It was while David was pondering his next move that he happened to run into fellow Dominican and baseball star Pedro Martinez.

Pedro was a star pitcher for the Boston Red Sox, and it was off one of his pitches that David had hit one of his more memorable homers during the 2002 season. As they got to talking, Pedro, the power pitcher, and David, the heavy hitter, mused about how great it would be if they played on the same team. This was likely just wistful thinking on David's part, but Pedro was determined to make it happen.

A short time later, Pedro began doing the rounds, calling up all the right people in order to get David on his team. And sure enough, David signed on with the Boston Red Sox for the 2003 season. During a Hall of Fame speech 20 years later, David recalled all of this and expressed his immense gratitude to Pedro Martinez for helping him during his time of need.

The 2003 season with the Red Sox was an incredible one that saw the team reach the playoffs, but they were ultimately bested by the New York Yankees. Even so, David told fans not to give up on him, pledging to take the Sox all the way to the World Series.

In 2004, he made good on that promise. He hit 41 home runs that season, and the Red Sox headed to the World Series, where they faced off against the St. Louis Cardinals. The Cardinals had been a formidable team that year, but Big Papi's bat made short work of them.

David Ortiz fulfilled his pledge, and the Red Sox were the World Series champions. It was the first time in several decades that the Sox had bagged a World Series win. The victory was just as spectacular as it was unexpected, and everyone agreed that it was all in large part to the considerable contributions of David Ortiz. When asked how he did it, David's answer was quite simple: He simply never stopped believing in himself.

He also gave a whole lot of credit to his teammate Pedro Martinez, without whose support he may not have returned to the big leagues at all. There would have been no Big Papi, and likely no 2004 World Series win for the Boston Red Sox. Stories like this just go to show how the kindness of one person can affect so many.

And as for how he got the name Big Papi? According to David, it all began because he had trouble remembering his teammates' names. If he couldn't remember someone's name, he would just call them Papi, which is a funny term of endearment among Dominicans. When Red Sox broadcaster Jerry Remy paid back the favor and referred to Ortiz as "Big Papi," the nickname was born.

FUN FACTS ABOUT DAVID ORTIZ!

- He's a 10 time All-Star.
- He gives to charity and founded the *David Ortiz Children's Fund*.
- He's a funny guy who has appeared in many funny commercials.
- He's one of the best "clutch" hitters of all time.
- David Ortiz became a US citizen on June 11th, 2008.

LEARN SOME DAVID ORTIZ TRIVIA!

What number was on David's jersey when he played for the Minnesota Twins?

Number 27!

How many World Series wins does Ortiz have?

Three!

What tattoo does David have on his arm?

The tattoo is of his mother, Angela.

What's David's favorite food?

Lobster (or any kind of seafood)!

Who First Called him Big Papi?

Red Sox Broadcaster Jerry Remy.

REAL-LIFE LESSONS FROM BIG PAPI!

- Never give up.
- Respect your elders.
- Be a team player.
- Have a sense of humor.
- Give back to the community.

Athletics

MARK MCGWIRE'S ON FIRE!

Mark McGwire was raised in a competitive family. His father, John, was himself an athlete, and a man well versed in how to overcome adversity. John had been struck with polio as a kid—an illness that had left him unable to fully use one of his legs. Even so, John grew up strong. He played baseball and golf, and even boxed when he got the chance.

It was from John that Mark and his four brothers learned the meaning of hard work and determination. John McGwire also passed down his love of sports.

Even though many of his peers might have been home playing their Ataris, Mark McGwire was out and about. There was never a dull moment growing up in his neighborhood in Pomona, California. If he wasn't at bat, he had a golf club, and if he wasn't putting, he was probably shooting hoops. Even so, Mark and his family and friends never took sports all that seriously. It was something they did to pass the time, but no one ever suspected that anyone in the McGwire household would become a Major League Baseball player.

Even so, word had gotten out about Mark's exploits. While he was still in high school, the Montreal Expos came calling. But Mark decided to delay his entry into professional baseball by going to college. Even though he loved baseball, he valued a college education and made his way to the University of Southern California.

Of course, along with taking his share of tests and writing all of those academic papers, he was still going to play ball. He joined the college baseball team and did his best to perfect his game while keeping up with his studies. His efforts paid off. By his junior year in college, he was once again being drafted by the big leagues. This time around, it was by the Oakland Athletics organization, better known by fans as the "Oakland A's." Not only would Mark not have to travel thousands of miles away to Montreal, he would also get to play for a team that was really going places.

Mark McGwire was presented with an even greater honor just prior to all of this, however, when he was picked to participate in the 1984 Olympics for the US baseball team. He would later look back fondly on the experience, stating that his participation was like fulfilling a lifelong dream.

Mark's Olympic dream team didn't do as well as expected, however, and he was frustrated to go home without a gold medal. Nevertheless, he was still a hot prospect for the Oakland A's. It was right after he came back from the Olympics that he began training with them.

Mark trained hard at the A's training grounds in Modesto, California. But as hard as he trained, his first season was a bit lackluster. It wasn't until his third official game that Mark finally found it within himself to rise to the occasion. That night, his team scored a clear victory, with the scoreboard reading 11 to 4.

But this was just the beginning. By 1987, Mark McGwire had obtained the coveted status of being named "Rookie of the Year." He had some competition on his own team, however, since the A's had yet another breakout star on their roster in the form of Jose Conseco.

The two power hitters would become fondly known as the "Bash Brothers" due to the way they bashed the ball across the field, as well as the friendly way they bashed their big biceps together when cheering each other on.

As Mark and Conseco kicked off the 1988 season, they soon realized how challenging it would be to top what they had achieved the previous year.

Mark McGwire just wasn't performing as well as he had in the past. He wasn't hitting the homers like he had before. Even so, the Oakland A's made it to the World Series, where they faced off against the Los Angeles Dodgers. Unfortunately, it was a contest that the Oakland A's were destined to lose.

Mark seemed to lose much of his joy for the game over the next couple of years. He just wasn't feeling it, and his dismal batting average seemed to bear witness to his displeasure. His 1991 season was so bad, in fact, that Mark found himself being taunted by elementary school children. His home in Alamo, California, just happened to be near the school, and the Little Leaguers there apparently knew all about his difficult season.

Mark later recalled that the kids would regularly walk to the fence that separated his yard from the school property to hurl insults. These kids apparently followed all the latest happenings in baseball, but now, instead of looking up to Mark as a role model, they were openly disparaging him.

Mark felt terrible. He even considered giving up baseball for good. But he didn't quit. Still, he didn't really rebound until the 1995 season. Interestingly, this was a shortened season due to a previous strike. Both the owners and players had gone on a generalized strike the previous year, due to disagreements between players unions and upper management. It was only when they realized that the strike was accomplishing nothing other than the alienation of their fans that it was called off in time for an abbreviated season in 1995.

Even though it was a shortened season, Mark went into it ready to go. He hit 39 home runs. The following season would be even better, with Mark hitting 50 home runs. Then, in 1997, he hit an astonishing 58 home runs. This was important, because it brought Mark ever closer to breaking the previous record held by baseball legend Roger Maris, who had bagged 61 homers in a single season.

The following season, in 1998, Mark once again found himself within striking distance of Maris' old record. But it wasn't for the A's. Rather, it was the Saint Louis Cardinals. Mark McGwire had been traded from the A's to the Cardinals, and perhaps that motivated him to go big and attempt to surpass that 61 home run record.

But he had company, for Chicago Cubs star Sammy Sosa was also a power hitter, and was close on his heels. By August, the two were tied at 47 home runs each.

Mark kept pulling ahead, and by September he was just short of Maris' old record, reaching 60 homers.

Mark ended up hitting his 61st homer of the season on September 7th, which just so happened to be his father's 61st birthday. Then, on the following day, September 8th, 1998, Mark McGwire hit his 62nd home run, beating Roger Maris' old record.

Although this record has since been topped by other ball players, it was Mark who led the way. For it was only after he beat the old Maris record, after 30 whole years of no one even coming close, that it began to seem possible. Mark McGwire showed what one could do if they put forth the effort.

FUN FACTS ABOUT MARK MCGWIRE!

- He played for Team USA in the 1985 Olympics.
- Mark won a Golden Glove award during the 1990 season.
- McGwire played college baseball for the USC Trojans.
- Part of I-70 is named after him.
- After retiring, he coached for the Cardinals.

LEARN SOME MARK MCGWIRE TRIVIA!

What's Mark's total home run count?

Mark McGwire hit a career total of 583 home runs.

What was Mark's longest home run?

He once hit a ball 545 feet, straight out of Busch Stadium.

What record did Mark McGwire break?

He broke Roger Maris' long-standing record for the number of home runs hit in a season.

Who was the second half of the Bash Brothers?

Jose Conseco.

How old was Mark when he hit his first homer?

It's said that Mark was only 8 years old when he first knocked a ball out of the park for his Little League team.

REAL-LIFE LESSONS FROM MARK MCGWIRE

- Dream big.
- Learn from others.
- Don't get discouraged.
- Stay grounded.
- Have confidence.

Astros

JUST KEEP ON TRYING THE STORY OF NOLAN RYAN

Although a lot of attention is given to the heavy hitters of baseball, there are some players who stand out not so much for their swing, but for their *throw*.

As soon as he stepped up to the mound, Nolan Ryan struck fear into the hearts of the batters he pitched to. Nolan was not just good—he was darn near perfect. He was one of the few pitchers gifted enough to throw multiple "no hitters."

This means that Nolan pitched entire games in which the opposing team was unable to hit the ball even one time. In 1991, he threw so many no hitters he was even congratulated by President George H. W. Bush, who sent him a telegram that simply read "Wow!"

By the early 1990s, Nolan was already a veteran in the game. His career dated back to the 1960s, when he first joined the league as a rookie with an amazing arm. Even back then, he was impressing folks with the speed and accuracy of his throw. He was like a machine, like an unstoppable train barreling down the tracks. It was for this reason that Nolan Ryan became known as "The Ryan Express."

But even before the Ryan Express became a thing, Nolan could be found throwing pitches for his high school team in his hometown of Alvin, Texas, where he played for the Alvin High School Yellowjackets. Here, the tall and lanky pitcher first learned how to strike out his opponents. It was during a high school game that he managed to catch the attention of a talent scout who worked for the New York Mets, a guy by the name of John Murff.

John—or Mr. Murff, as young Nolan likely called him—was shocked at the ease with which Nolan handled the baseball. He could see that the expert manner in which the player was able to control both the speed and direction of the ball seemed to strike terror in the hearts of those who were at bat for the opposing team.

They struggled to try and hit his pitches, and the more pitches they missed, the more frustrated and erratic their own batting became. These folks had just unwittingly boarded the Ryan Express, with a one-way ticket back to the dugout!

Nolan would throw solid pitches that were fair throws, yet the ball moved so fast that the batters would still miss them. Once the batters were a bit shaken up and unsteady due to the misses, Nolan would then change things up and purposely throw a curveball, knowing that the unsteady batters, eager to correct their previous mistakes, would *overcorrect* and take the bait, swinging and missing at the deceptively curved pitch.

Mr. Murff was so impressed with what he saw that he went back to New York and told the Mets all about it. He was given the go-ahead to court this talented prospect. After getting to know Nolan, John Murff discovered that, although still relatively young, the boy had practically been born playing the game.

Born on January 31st, 1947, Nolan grew up with a natural inclination to throw things. A lot of kids throw tantrums, but Nolan Ryan *threw stuff*. One of his favorite pastimes was throwing rocks! He and his little friends would go out to the swampy bayou near where they lived and arm themselves with rocks, which they would throw at the deadly water moccasins that were lurking nearby! These were venomous snakes that lived in the bayou.

This is where Nolan first perfected his throwing arm, learning to hit all of those snakes!

It wasn't until he was 9 years old that Nolan traded rocks for baseballs by joining the local Little League team. Along with baseball, however, he also found a passion for dodgeball, or "bombardment," as it was referred to in his Texas school.

No one wanted to get bombarded by the throwing arm of young Nolan Ryan! As soon as the coach blew the whistle and the kids started grabbing balls to throw at their opponents, all bets were off! Nolan would leave a stinging impression on anyone who fell into his line of sight while he was wielding a dodgeball! It's said that the opposing players would quickly seek the far corners of the gymnasium to get away from Nolan, but his powerful throws could still reach them

Scouts never know what they might run into when popping up at a random high school or college game. They typically see a bunch of wannabes and mediocre players, but there was no denying the raw talent of Nolan Ryan. He was already throwing no hitters, and during his senior year of high school, he helped the Yellowjackets make it all the way to the state tournament.

This was enough to get old Murff moving, and soon Nolan was being offered a $30,000 contract to play for the New York Mets. Nolan Ryan could hardly believe it, and neither could his parents! That was a lot of money back then. It was more than his father typically made in a whole year.

Nolan felt conflicted about it. He was genuinely excited at the chance to play Major League baseball, but he was also young and unsure if he was ready for such a commitment. Can you imagine what it would be like to be a teenager who has just been given a ticket to leave home and go thousands of miles away to a strange, new place you had never been to? That's what Nolan's contract amounted to.

Thanks to Mr. Murff, Nolan had a ticket to New York. But he knew that homesickness for Texas wouldn't be far behind. He also knew that he had other dreams besides baseball. He loved animals and had expressed an early interest in either being a veterinarian or a cattle farmer.

Accepting this contract with the New York Mets, as incredible as it might be, seemed to mark an end to any other possible career for Nolan. This was a pretty big decision for a young person to make, and it weighed heavily on the teenager's shoulders. Nevertheless, with the encouragement of his friends and family, he signed on the dotted line.

It was the summer of 1965, and for 18-year-old Nolan Ryan, life was just beginning. He was soon on a plane, not to New York, but to Virginia, where the Mets' Minor League team was training. Nolan Ryan had never flown on a plane before, and would later admit having all kinds of jitters during the course of that first flight.

Nevertheless, he was ready to go as soon as he hit the field, and by his 1966 season he was regularly striking out batters. Of course, it wasn't always an easy run for him. At one point, he was injured, causing him to sit out a few games. Nevertheless, he still managed to rise to prominence, just in time for the 1969 World Series, where he faced off against the Baltimore Orioles.

The pivotal moment in the series came when Nolan Ryan ascended the pitcher's mound, ready to pitch, just as the bases were loaded. This is a term used in baseball that means that there is a player on first, second, and third base, all seeking to score. The Orioles had a man on each base, and one of their best batters, Paul Blair, was ready to knock the ball out of the park. By doing so, he and all of his other teammates on base would be able to benefit from a home run, scoring a total of four points.

It was up to Ryan to try and prevent this from happening. He had to strike Paul Blair out. He threw some fast balls and managed to cause the power hitter to miss the first two pitches. In baseball, you are out after three strikes, so all he needed to do was throw one more good pitch and Paul would be done for.

Blair was expecting another fast ball and was trying to compensate for it, but instead of a fast ball, Ryan switched things up by throwing a curve. If Paul had realized as much, he could have pulled his punches and not swung, but since he was already rattled by the two previous fast balls, he swung almost on reflex, and as that ball curved wildly away from him, he found himself hitting nothing but air. With this triumph of Nolan Ryan's pitching arm, the Mets went on to win the World Series.

Nolan was happy to win one for New York, but he never really adjusted to life in the big city and was soon clamoring for a trade to somewhere a little more to his liking. This trade came in 1971, when he was sent off to play for the Angels in California.

Nolan wasn't all that thrilled at first. The Angels didn't have a very good record at the time and they were largely being made to play second fiddle to another major California team—the Los Angeles Dodgers. Nolan Ryan had bigger problems, however, when the team decided to go on strike. Nolan had gotten married, and he and his wife now had a young son to take care of.

Nolan became disillusioned with what was happening, and the more he sat it out during the strike, the more he was tempted to just give up baseball entirely. But he just couldn't give up quit. He was determined to stick it out, and with his wife Ruth's encouragement, that's exactly what he did. He waited out the strike, and was soon back out on the pitcher's mound doing his best to strike everybody else out.

By 1973, he was doing so well that he was on the verge of breaking a record. Famed pitcher Sandy Koufax had thrown 382 strikeouts during one season, and by late September of 1973, Nolan was just a handful of strikeouts away from surpassing Sandy's record.

During a faceoff against the Minnesota Twins, Nolan Ryan achieved his dream. He struck out Twins batter Rich Reese and set the record. But he soon broke another record, this time for the speed of a baseball. The fastest ball had previously been thrown back in 1946, by a player named Bob Feller. Bob had thrown a ball that clocked in at 98.6 miles an hour, but Nolan was determined to beat this record, and beat it he did. Pitching to a White Sox batter, he threw a ball that was clocked at 101.8 miles an hour. And this wasn't even the fastest ball thrown by Nolan—there would be much faster pitches to come.

Despite his records, his days in California were numbered due to disagreements over his contract. He was eventually let go and went looking for another team. The team that ended up taking him home was one that was indeed *close to home*, for it was none other than Texas' own Houston Astros.

For Nolan Ryan, this move was truly a homecoming. From the very start of his time with the Astros, in December of 1979, he made it clear to fans that there was no place like home. And it certainly didn't hurt that 32-year-old Nolan Ryan was being paid well. He was being given a hefty $1 million salary for his trouble.

He began the year on a roll, and carried his momentum into subsequent seasons. In 1981, he achieved a no hitter victory against his old foes the LA Dodgers. This was a stunning victory in itself, but even more so since it was the fifth no-hitter of his career, which broke the previous record held by Sandy Koufax.

Now was now in his mid-30s, but he still had more no hitters to come. In the meantime, he was also trying to beat the all time strikeout record. Nolan He reached this milestone in the 1983 season, during a game against the Montreal Expos.

Nolan eventually moved on from the Houston Astros, going to the Texas Rangers in 1989, where he continued to abide by a strict work ethic.

He was known as a bit of a health nut and fitness fanatic. When he wasn't practicing his throwing arm, he pursued marathon sessions on an exercise bike. To outside spectators, he may not have seemed like he was going anywhere on the stationary bike, but in his mind, he knew that he was keeping himself in top shape so that he could continue to take the baseball world by storm.

During the 1990s, when he was well into his 40s, Nolan was still knocking them dead with no hitters. He never ceased to give it his all. This should be a lesson to all of us that if we put in the effort and keep trying, we can do anything we set our hearts and minds to.

FUN FACTS ABOUT NOLAN RYAN!

- He's a World Series champ.
- He's an 8 time All-Star.
- He struck out 5,714 batters.
- Nolan Ryan threw 7 no hitters.
- Yet...He Never Pitched a Perfect Game (A perfect game is a game in which the opposing team is not able to reach any bases. This means that not only are there no hits, but also no walks, no hit batsmen, no uncaught third strikes, no fielder or catcher interference, and no fielding errors. The game has to be perfect.

LEARN SOME NOLAN RYAN TRIVIA!

What was Nolan Ryan's high school?

Alvin High School.

How long did Nolan's Major League baseball career last?

27 seasons.

Who else is on Nolan Ryan's Rookie Card?

He appears alongside pitcher Jerry Koosman.

What's Nolan's full name?

His full name is Lynn Nolan Ryan Jr.

What is Nolan Ryan's side hustle?

He's a cattle rancher!

REAL-LIFE LESSONS FROM NOLAN RYAN!

- Practice makes perfect.
- Don't forget your roots.
- Do your best.
- Know your strengths and weaknesses.
- Seize opportunity.

GRIFFEY
24

KEN GRIFFEY JR. FOLLOWING IN HIS FATHER'S FOOTSTEPS

Ken Griffey Jr. was born on November 21st, 1969. He was the son of his namesake, Ken Griffey Sr., and his wife Alberta. Griffey Jr.'s father was himself a top-rate baseball player who was hammering it out for the Cincinnati Reds when his son came into the world. Inspired by the success of his dad on the field, Ken Griffey Jr. couldn't wait until he was old enough to join a Little League team.

By the time he was just 8 years old, Ken Griffey Jr. was a rising star in the Little Leagues, known for being a tremendous pitcher and a fantastic outfielder. Meanwhile, his father was eventually traded from the Reds to the New York Yankees. The Yankees had always been an outstanding team, and this was a great opportunity for Ken Griffey Sr.

The only trouble was, his family had to stay behind in Cincinnati. This meant that his wife and kids—including aspiring baseballer Ken Griffey Jr.—had to make due without their dad around.

Fortunately, Jr.'s father had taught him to be strong, and he was motivated enough to be a self-starter. Plus, he knew that if he ever really needed his dad's advice, he was just a phone call away. And if he really needed some one-on-one time with his dear old dad, Ken Griffey Sr. would fly him to New York. Not many kids have a dad who can buy plane tickets on the spur of the moment, but Ken Griffey Jr. most certainly did.

According to the younger Griffey, his father would simply put him on another flight the very next day and send him home. Just like that, Ken Griffey Jr. would be back in Cincinnati ready to get back to baseball, school, or whatever else he was doing, without missing a beat.

Ken Jr. improved his game as a young teenager, and soon had scouts looking into his potential future in the big leagues. The scouts came calling when Ken Griffey Jr. was only 14 years old. During this time, he was playing ball in Cincinnati—not for the Reds, but for Archbishop Moeller High School. Moeller is an exclusive prep school that has had many notable breakout stars, such as Barry Larkin, Buddy Bell, and Brent Suter.

Griffey Jr. was a star baseball player and an incredible football player during his time at Moeller. Football was actually more convenient for father/son time, since football season just so happened to start when baseball season was coming to a close. Football starts in the fall, right when sluggers like Ken Griffey Sr. are hanging up their bats.

By Ken Griffey Jr.'s senior year, he had decided to put all of his energy into baseball. He realized that there was no way he could do his best at both sports, and his natural strengths were on the baseball field.

Ken Griffey Jr. made this decision in 1986, and he was soon on a clear trajectory to follow in his dad's footsteps. He ramped up his efforts in 1987, and managed to get drafted by the Mariners, who made his contract official on June 2nd, 1987. A few days later, he walked across the graduation stage at Moeller High.

Soon, this 17-year-old prodigy was heading off for Bellingham, Washington, some 90 miles north of Seattle, where perfected his game with the Bellingham Mariners. The Bellingham Mariners are a Minor League team affiliated with the Seattle Mariners. Ken

Griffey Jr. was a hot prospect, and he didn't disappoint. During his first season, he was recognized as the Northwest League Player of the Week. That's a great distinction for anyone—let alone a guy who was still in high school a few weeks earlier!

Considering how young he was, it shouldn't be surprising that Ken Griffey Jr. began to get a little homesick. He would later reflect that missing his old stomping grounds in Ohio was one of the biggest challenges he faced. This homesickness grew after Griffey Jr. sustained a bad injury to his shoulder on July 4th of that year. He had rammed his shoulder into the outfield wall while running down a ball. This had him on the benches for the next several days while he recovered, and was a tough break for the young player, who spent most of his down time calling his friends and family back home in Cincinnati.

Griffey Jr. began sliding into depression during this period. But even when he visited home, he couldn't quite overcome the dark thoughts that were hounding him. He was under too much pressure to succeed, and also felt entirely uncertain about the future and what he should do with the rest of his life, and he eventually had a bit of a nervous breakdown. Things came to a head during holiday break in Cincinnati, when Ken Griffey Jr. rang in the New Year of 1988 by swallowing a bottle of aspirin. It's not clear what was going on in his mind, but this was most certainly a cry for help.

It's unfortunate and frightening, but there are times when folks feel so desperate about the situations that they find themselves in that they end up making bad decisions. This is especially the case if someone feels their situation is hopeless and they have no one to whom they can voice their problems.

Although he had friends and family he could talk to, Ken Griffey Jr. felt isolated. All of those phone calls to Cincinnati weren't enough for him to fully express himself. He felt like no one was listening to him, and that there was no one he could really talk to about how sad he felt inside. Without any outlet to voice his concerns, this young man sadly turned toward self-destructive behavior to get his point across.

If decisive action hadn't been taken, Ken Griffey Jr. could have been in serious trouble. Fortunately, he was taken to the hospital in time to have his stomach pumped, and was given proper treatment to fully recover. His father was very upset, and as soon as his son was awake and cognizant enough to understand what he was saying, he didn't hesitate to lecture him about the ramifications of his actions.

Ultimately, both father and son came to realize that Ken Jr. was just feeling like he was under too much pressure. The best thing for him, at this point, was to take it easy and blow off some steam. All of us can feel overwhelmed at times, and Ken Jr. learned that instead of bottling all of those feelings up, it's best to openly talk them out. That's a good lesson for all of us to learn.

With the support of his friends and family, Ken Griffey Jr. was able to recover. Upon returning to the field the following season, he had a renewed determination not just to do well in baseball, but to also keep himself balanced on an emotional level. He was determined to do his best, without making himself feel overwhelmed in the process. His efforts were noted, and he was finally bumped up to the big leagues, signing on with the Seattle Mariners for the 1989 season. Since his dad was still playing in the Majors at the time, the two made history as the first father-and-son duo in the Major Leagues.

One of the first teams Ken Griffey Jr. squared off against was the legendary Oakland A's. The A's had two star players at the time: Mark McGuire and Jose Conseco, otherwise known as the "Bash Brothers." But during a home game in Seattle however, 19-year-old Ken Griffey Jr. showed that he could bash the ball with the best of them when he hit a home run of his own out of left field.

In the early 1990s, the world truly got to see Ken Griffey Jr. shine. In the 1990 season in particular, he really came into his own. His stunning catches became legendary. As much as home runs might be celebrated, the guy that manages to catch balls that *could have been home runs is* just as incredible. Griffey Jr. had the ability to practically climb the back walls of the outfield in order to grab these would-be homers. He did this on one occasion in particular, when he halfway mounted the wall and raised his glove well above it in order to catch a ball that otherwise would have been a homer. This rare feat has since been termed "robbing a home run." But there's nothing duplicitous about Ken Griffey Jr.'s game, it's just pure and unadulterated skill.

Meanwhile, Ken Griffey Sr. wasn't having the best of seasons with the Cincinnati Reds. His stats were low, with just 62 at-bats, 8 RBIs, and only one measly home run. He ended up being traded to the Mariners, which created another historic moment. The fact that both Griffey's were now on the same team became the biggest news in the world of baseball.

Many wondered how much longer the legendary Ken Griffey Sr., who was now in his 40s, would be able to play, even as they cheered his up-and-coming son Ken Griffey Jr. It was going to be an interesting season for the Mariners, to say the least. Ken Griffey Jr. tried to play off the hype joking that it wasn't a big deal. It would be just like "playing catch with Dad in the backyard."

Griffey Sr. had dropped in on the Mariners right in the middle of his son's incredible 1990 season, and he enjoyed it so much that he decided to return for the 1991 season, as well. The two had an absolute blast together. Realizing he couldn't beat the experience he'd had with his son, Ken Griffey Sr. decided to quit while he was on top and retired at the end of the 1991 season. Ken Griffey Jr., in the meantime, enjoyed a long and incredible baseball career that lasted all the way to 2010.

FUN FACTS ABOUT KEN GRIFFEY JR.

- He's a recipient of the coveted Golden Glove award.
- His father, Ken Griffey Sr., retired at 41.
- Ken Griffey Jr. was drafted right out of high school.
- Griffey Jr. and Griffey Sr. both played for the Mariners.
- He has a younger brother named Craig.

LEARN SOME KEN GRIFFEY JR. TRIVIA!

When was Ken Griffey Jr. born?

He was born on November 21st, 1969.

Who was Ken Griffey Jr.'s mom?

Alberta Griffey.

What's Griffey Jr.'s full name?

George Kenneth Griffey Jr.

What 1990s cartoon portrayed Ken Griffey Jr.?

The Simpsons.

What's his hometown?

Cincinnati, Ohio.

REAL-LIFE LESSONS FROM KEN GRIFFEY JR.!

- Work hard.
- Be a team player.
- Learn from others who came before you.
- Pick yourself up when you fall.
- Don't be afraid to ask for help.

I have included these free downloadable gifts to help light up your inner inspiration & reach your potential.

While you are reading through the stories, lessons and trivia, we recommend that you make use of all the bonuses we've attached here!

All our bonuses have been made specifically to help young athletes feel fired up, get inspired from the best to ever do it, and most importantly fall more in love with this incredible game!

Here's a list of what you're getting:

1) 250 Fun Facts From The World Of Sports
2) Sports Practice and Game Calendar
3) 5 Fun Exercise Drills for Kids
4) The BEST Advice From The Greatest Athletes Of All Time
5) The Mental Mindset Guided Meditation & Affirmation Collection
6) The Most Famous Events In Sports History And What They Can Teach Us

Now, it's over to you to scan the QR code, follow the instructions & get started!

SOME REAL-LIFE LESSONS FROM DEREK JETER

During his time playing for the New York Yankees, Derek Jeter earned the title of "Captain." This wasn't some sort of military lingo—what it meant was that Derek was simply so good, he was quite naturally considered the leader of the team.

Jeter was born on June 26th, 1974. Although his father hailed from the deep south in Alabama, he was born in his mother's native New Jersey, and it would be the East Coast of his maternal relatives that he would come to most identify with in life. He spent a lot of time with his maternal grandma, who also lived in New Jersey, and whom Derek fondly referred to as "Gram."

His grandma later recalled Derek's early obsession with baseball, and how he would frequently pull her to the side to announce, "Come on, Gram! Let's throw!" Along with occasionally playing catch, Gram also indulged her grandson by taking him to see what ultimately became his team—The New York Yankees.

His parents had made a good home for their son, not in Alabama or New Jersey, but somewhere sort of in between—Kalamazoo, Michigan. Here, he made a name for himself as a phenomenal athlete. By the time he was in high school, he was a clear standout player. During his senior year he was named National High School Player of the Year. Soon, scouts started taking notice and he began getting offers.

All the while, Derek still made sure to make As and Bs in the classroom. His grades and obvious prowess on the field enabled him to snag a generous scholarship from the University of Michigan. The only trouble was that, shortly thereafter, he was also offered a direct draft into the Major League by the team he idolized—The New York Yankees!

He was obviously very excited at the prospects of playing for the Yankees, but at the same time, he didn't want to miss out on a college education. However, he finally decided to go for the Yankees' offer, since he determined that he could play pro ball and then use the money he earned to go to school in his spare time. He figured he would be playing ball and cramming for tests in college baseball anyway, so why not play for the pros and go to class at the same time? So it was that Derek Jeter found himself on his way to the pros.

The first year was a tough transition. He had never been on his own before, and suddenly there he was with the Yankees, fending for himself. He started to have his doubts, and began to wonder if perhaps he had made a mistake. Would he have been better off going to Michigan University and playing college ball? These were the sorts of questions he asked himself. He just couldn't help but second guess his decision.

He was soon shipped off to a training camp in Greensboro, and his feelings of homesickness only grew worse. These feelings seemed to show up in the 1993 season, when he began to make some rather sloppy errors. He corrected them by the end of the season, and actually managed to get moved to a more prestigious farming camp located in Columbus. All of this soon led to Derek being named Player of the Year.

This was all part of the build up toward Derek making the official Yankees team in New York, which finally happened in 1995. During the 1995 season, he was tasked with replacing an injured player—Tony Fernandez. Then, in 1996, Derek was made the main shortstop for the team. In baseball, a shortstop is one of the most important defensive positions.

It is located right in the middle of the field, between third and second base, where all of the action is. Whoever plays shortstop essentially becomes a manager of momentum in the infield, making sure that the ball gets where it needs to go. Since the guy playing shortstop has to command so much of the action, he is often named captain of the team.

This is how Derek became captain of the Yankees, and he soon proved to be especially suited for the role. He did his best to up his defensive game, and was soon one of the most effective shortstops the Yankees ever had. Being a great shortstop might not be as glamorous as being a strike-out pitcher or a home run hitter, but if you do your best, no matter the position you are given, it will eventually show.

That's precisely what Derek Jeter did, and he was soon considered one of the best shortstops in the league. Shortstop is a defensive position strategically located between 2nd and 3rd base. The shortstop is tasked with thwarting offensive plays, as well as being on the lookout for attempts to steal bases.

Derek Jeter continued to lead the Yankees as their shortstop and captain, taking them all the way to the World Series in 2009, where they were victorious against the Philadelphia Phillies.

Shortstop is not the most glamorous position, but it gets the job done. Derek has credited the sense of modesty instilled in him during his upbringing with his willingness to try and do well at all aspects of baseball, rather than just focusing on the flashier roles.

He insists that his folks raised him with the idea that he shouldn't take anything for granted, and that he should try to do well no matter what role he was given. That should be a lesson to us all.

No matter where we find ourselves in life, we should always strive
to do our very best.

FUN FACTS ABOUT DEREK JETER!

- He was born in New Jersey.
- He grew up in Michigan.
- In high school he was named National High School Player of the Year.
- In 2014 he was on an All-Star team with Mike Trout.
- He has numerous endorsements, such as Nike, Ford, Visa, and Subway.

LEARN SOME DEREK JETER TRIVIA!

What was Derek Jeter's last season?

He last played in 2014.

What videogame is based on Derek Jeter?

Derek Jeter Pro Baseball 2008.

What's Derek's favorite food?

Pancakes and an omelet! He eats it every morning!

What classic sitcom did Derek appear on?

He made a cameo appearance on *Seinfeld*.

REAL-LIFE LESSONS FROM DEREK JETER!

- Don't take anything for granted.
- Listen to your parents.
- Hone your skills.
- Work hard.
- Be kind.

IANTS

GAME ON WITH BARRY BONDS

Barry Bonds—the homerun king—was one of the most dynamic baseball players to ever grace the field. His 2001 season was one of his best, for it was during this season that he broke the all-time home run record previously set by slugger Mark McGwire, who hit 70 homers in a single season. Barry hit 73.

The power hitter was born on July 24th, 1964, in the quaint confines of Riverside, California. He was the oldest kid in his family, and had three younger siblings. Barry's parents, Bobby and Pat, expected a lot from their eldest son. Above all, they wanted him to be a good example for his siblings.

Barry had his own set of idols to look up to. An avid sports fan since childhood, he looked up to old baseball greats such as Mickey Mantle and Willie Mays, as well as the basketball phenom Kareem Abdul-Jabbar. He also idolized his own father, Bobby, who was himself a baseball player. Bobby played alongside the legendary Willie Mays on the San Francisco Giants.

This was the same team that Barry would end up playing for after he was drafted in 1993. Prior to this, Barry played baseball in college, for Arizona State University.

Barry was known as a good all-around player, and fans were particularly enthusiastic about his ability to steal bases. While stealing is wrong in most other areas in life, it is perfectly legal in the game of baseball. In baseball, teams have to always be on their guard to make sure the players of the opposing teams don't sneak to another base while they are preoccupied.

Barry was a master at finding just the right opportunity to quickly dash to the next base before the ball could be tossed his way. He had first perfected this skill when he was playing college baseball for Arizona State. During this time, he hooked up with one of his father's old buddies, Oakland A's superstar Rickey Henderson.

Back when Barry was in college, the Oakland A's had a training facility in Arizona, not far from Barry's school. He would regularly visit the training facility, where Rickey showed Barry how to steal bases. He taught Barry that the key was to focus on the mannerisms of the pitcher. Rickey said that it was especially important to focus on the pitcher's eyes. By doing so, one could know where he was about to throw the ball, and find the best opportunities to steal a base.

After he finished college, Barry was drafted by the Pirates in 1985. He kicked off his first season with the team in 1986. Barry had always liked the Pirates as a team, as some of his favorite players, such as Willie Stargell and Roberto Clemente, were Pirates. His big debut for the team came in May of 1986, when he played center field in a game against the LA Dodgers. When he finally got his chance at bat, his performance was a bit disappointing. He hit the ball, but it was a pop-up that was fielded by the shortstop. The rest of the team's performance was also rather lackluster, and the Pirates went on to lose the game. But Barry Bonds was not one to be discouraged easily.

The following year, during the 1987 season, Barry really showed the world of baseball what he could do. He began hitting home runs and stealing bases left and right. But then Bonds came up against someone he had never faced before.

He found himself staring down the pitching arm of famed no hitter Nolan Ryan! Nolan was known for fast balls that could strike the best batters out, and Barry was no exception. The first time he faced off against Nolan in a game, he struck out three times.

Bonds was shocked and dismayed at these results, but he once again drew upon that source of inner strength he had been nurturing since his youth, and willed himself to try even harder.

The 1988 season saw Barry riding high, but the 1989 season turned into a terrible slump for the breakout star. He got married and began raising a family, so distractions from his personal life might have played a role in Barry taking his eyes off the ball.

Fortunately, by the 1990 season, he was back in top form. He did so well, in fact, that he was named to the National League All-Star team. The Pirates made their way to the playoffs, but ultimately fell short. Despite that fact, Barry was named MVP.

Barry's 1991 season was also phenomenal, which is why it might have come as a surprise when the decision was made to trade the star player in the middle of 1992.

But there were some things going on behind the scenes that weren't so pretty. Barry was never the darling of the press, like many other players. He tended to be aloof and kept to himself. Many in the media interpreted his aloofness as being mean spirited, stuck up, or even arrogant.

This perception was heavily reinforced due to an incident in 1991, when photographers who had permission to photograph a Pirates practice found themselves being shouted down and berated by Barry Bonds. Barry apparently wasn't in a good mood and didn't want to have his picture taken. The problem was that it wasn't his decision to make. The photographers had been commissioned to take pictures of the practice, and as long as Barry was in uniform and on the field, he was considered fair game, just like every other player. But try telling that to Barry Bonds!

After the shouting match with the photographers, the Pirates staff pulled him to the side and tried to explain the situation to him, but Barry was still irate. Barry's behavior reached the ears of Pirates manager Jim Leyland, and he was not pleased. He was so upset, in fact, that he began openly considering giving Barry the boot.

This just goes to show you that no matter how good you might be at a sport or anything else in life, if you act like a complete jerk, you can put your future in jeopardy! Barry Bonds learned this lesson the hard way.

After the Pirates cut ties with Barry, he signed a contract with the San Francisco Giants. He signed on as a free agent, with a hefty $43 million. Now he was playing for the team that his father had retired with.

From this point forward, Barry tried to develop a more favorable image with the press. It didn't always work, but he had learned a valuable lesson when it came to good sportsmanship and generally good behavior. These are lessons that we can all learn from.

FUN FACTS ABOUT
BARRY BONDS!

- He was born on July 24th, 1964.
- Barry's father Bobby was also a baseball player.
- Barry Bonds was mentored by Rickey Henderson.
- He was struck out by Nolan Ryan.
- He had a complicated relationship with the media.

LEARN SOME
BARRY BONDS TRIVIA!

Who were Barry Bonds' favorite baseball players growing up?

Willie Mays, Roberto Clemente, and Mickey Mantle.

How many World Series rings does Barry Bonds have?

None.

What's Barry's favorite cartoon character?

In college, he was known to enjoy watching He-Man!

What's Barry's favorite food?

It's said he loves a good plate of chicken and waffles.

Who was Barry's godfather?

None other than Willie Mays!

REAL-LIFE LESSONS
FROM BARRY BONDS!

- Practice makes perfect.
- Follow great examples.
- Maintain a good sense of humor.
- Learn to keep a cool head.
- Don't sweat the small stuff.

KEEPING IT SIMPLE WITH MARIANO RIVERA'S "MIRACLE" PITCH!

During his time with the New York Yankees, Mariano Rivera was celebrated as the "Closer." But before being recruited by New York, Mariano was born on November 29th, 1960, in the Central American nation of Panama. His father worked on a fishing boat, and his mother did her best to take care of Mariano and his siblings.

Mariano grew up assuming that he, too, would one day fish—or, perhaps, if he was lucky, become a mechanic. He loved to work on stuff, and had a great aptitude for taking things apart and putting them back together. But all that changed when he was introduced to a baseball recruiter from the United States. The recruiter discovered that Mariano was quite a ball player, and soon asked him to sign a contract to play for the New York Yankees.

Mariano later admitted that he barely even understood what this meant at the time. It was only after the scout explained that he would be flown out to the United States to play for a Major League baseball team that the gravity of the situation finally sunk in. It was both a frightening and exciting prospect to leave behind everything he knew to play Major League baseball in the US.

He had to think it over, but with the encouragement of his friends and family, he finally decided to sign the contract. Shortly thereafter, 20-year-old Mariano plunked down in the back of his dad's Nissan pickup truck and was driven to the airport. He flew to the US and began training with a Yankees Minor League team in Florida.

Mariano bounced around the Minors for a while before making the main Yankees Major League team in New York in 1995. He made his debut that May, when the Yankees faced off against the Los Angeles Angels. He did well enough, and soon there was quite a buzz about the Panamanian newbie. However there were still some skeptics in the Yankees' upper management who were not entirely sure that Mariano had what it took.

Their skepticism ended when some of his pitches that summer were clocked at 96 miles per hour. This was much faster than his previous speed, and came as a shock. No one was sure how he was suddenly pitching such fast balls, but Mariano had an interesting explanation—he said it was thanks to God!

Some might have laughed at such remarks, but Mariano wasn't joking. He was a firm believer in the Christian faith and truly believed that God was working in his life. He ended up attributing his unique pitching style to the Almighty. This supposed divine intervention occurred during the 1997 season, when Mariano was pitching to fellow Yankee Ramiro Mendoza and his pitch began to move in an odd cutting motion. The ball would cut to the side just as Mendoza tried to catch it. At first, the pitch was a bit annoying to them both, but the more Mariano threw it, the more they realized that he just might be onto something.

As difficult as this cutting pitch was for Ramiro to catch, it was exceedingly more difficult for any batter to hit! What Mariano had stumbled upon was a very rare pitching style, the so-called "fast cutter," sometimes referred to as a "cut fastball." It's a fastball that cuts to the side at the last moment. Not many pitchers can master the technique, yet Mariano seemed to have stumbled upon it at random.

Mariano dubbed it his "miracle pitch" and later stated his belief that it was divine providence at work. Whatever the case may be, Mariano and his pitch became a reliable fixture of the New York Yankees.

Mariano believed in God, and in himself—and everything else fell right into place. As Mariano himself once put it, "I feel like God is on my side and will help me deal with anything."

Mariano has a good sense of control and is known for his ability to be cool under pressure. Whether on the mound or in everyday life, he keeps his composure. "I don't get nervous," Mariano says. "I trust God." That ability to tap into a great source of power should be a great lesson to us all.

FUN FACTS ABOUT MARIANO RIVERA!

- Mariano was born in Panama.
- His dad caught fish for a living.
- Mariano once dreamed of becoming a mechanic.
- He's nicknamed the "Closer."
- He's a man of deep faith.

LEARN SOME MARIANO RIVERA TRIVIA!

When did Mariano become a US citizen?

He became an official citizen in 2015.

How many World Series wins does Mariano have?

Mariano has five World Series wins under his belt.

When was he born?

November 29th, 1969.

What's Mariano's favorite food?

He loves chocolate milk. In fact, it's said that he was always sure to drink some chocolate milk before every game!

What article of Mariano's clothing was put on display in a museum?

His cleats from the 1999 World Series are part of an exhibit at the National Baseball Hall of Fame and Museum.

REAL-LIFE LESSONS FROM MARIANO RIVERA!

- Have faith.
- Tap into your own inner strength.
- Trust in yourself.
- Help your teammates.
- Trust in God.

MR. CONSECUTIVE CAL RIPKEN JR. AND THE ART OF SHOWING UP!

Cal Ripken Jr. was born on August 24th, 1960, to Cal Sr. and his wife Violet. He grew up in the state of Maryland, where he was surrounded by folks just as dedicated to work as they were to play. During his off time, his dad wouldn't hesitate to pull out the baseball and mitt, so that he and his son could play catch.

Cal Ripken Sr. actually played baseball in the Minors for the Baltimore Orioles. When his son was born, Cal Sr. seemed on his way to the Majors. But an incident in 1961 saw him hit in the shoulder by a wild ball, and the injury put an end to these dreams. His shoulder was dinged so bad that it affected his best asset—his throwing arm.

A short time later, Cal Ripken Sr. decided to leave the Orioles and work full time as a baseball coach. Even though he couldn't play ball himself, he had enough knowledge to teach others—so that's exactly what he did. It wasn't easy for his wife and kids, however, since they often had to travel with Cal Sr. while he was on the road with the teams he coached.

Cal Jr. remembered bouncing from town to town, as his dad coached. The cities were all different, but the baseball was the same. Eventually, the baseball diamond became like a second home for Cal Ripken Jr.

Cal Ripken Jr. embraced the game just as much as his father, and soon joined a Little League team. He played well enough to take his team to the state championship when he was just 13 years old. His skills gained the attention of Earl Weaver, who became the manager of the Orioles a couple of years later.

Soon, the Orioles had Cal Jr. come down for a tryout, and they ultimately drafted him in 1978. He was drafted right out of high school.

Some players struggle when they have to decide whether or not to go to the pros or to college, but for Cal Ripken Jr. it wasn't a problem at all. He thought that if he was good enough, it would work out in the Majors, and if not, he could always go back to school later. So it was that a teenaged Cal Ripken Jr. found himself playing for the Orioles with a bunch of players much older than him.

The team he first played for was the Bluefield Orioles, located in Bluefield, West Virginia, which was a Minor League variant of the main Orioles franchise. Orioles fans liked to call the team the "Baby Birds." Even in the Minor Leagues, however, Cal Jr. soon noticed the big difference between professional ball and high school ball. He was up for the challenge, and worked himself hard to get up to speed.

In the meantime, he made some great friends and ended up getting a place with a few of his teammates. He became roomies with fellow Orioles players Larry Sheets, Tim Norris, and Mike Boddicker. These guys spent a lot of time together. When they weren't on the field playing baseball, they were at home playing cards.

Cal Ripken Jr.'s big break came in August of 1981, when he was given a spot on the Baltimore Orioles' Major League team. Going from the Minors to the Majors is a thrill for anyone, and Cal could hardly contain his enthusiasm.

He was placed in the infield, where he did everything he could to stand out. He opened up the 1982 season by literally knocking the ball out of the park. The 21-year-old impressed fans with a home run that allowed the Orioles to win the day. But a short time later, Cal Jr. hit some setbacks and had to sit on the bench for much of the rest of the 1982 season.

In 1983, everything changed. Cal had a truly outstanding season. He and his team took it all the way to the World Series, where they faced off against the Philadelphia Phillies. Cal was ready to go, and was especially excited to learn that President Ronald Reagan would be in attendance on the opening night of the series.

Perhaps Cal had a bad case of the jitters with the president looking over his shoulder, because the Orioles ended up getting trounced by the Phillies that night. Nevertheless, the team rallied and was able to come back against the Phillies with a vengeance, beating them in the next few games of the series. They triumphed in the end and became that year's World Series champs. In addition, Cal Ripken Jr. was named MVP.

At the start of the 1984 season, Cal Ripken Jr. hit the ground running. His offense and defense were both impeccable, but a team is more than one persona, and the team as a whole lagged behind. The Baltimore Orioles ended up in fifth place and failed to make the World Series that year.

By this point, Cal had a steady workout routine unrivaled by any. He wanted to be consistent more than anything else, and he realized that, in order to have consistency, he would need to have a dedicated workout and training routine that helped him stay in tip-top shape.

He also had what his teammates referred to as a certain "mental toughness." That toughness was on full display during a 1985 game when he badly sprained his ankle, yet forced himself to limp through the entire game. The pain was so bad that many would have sat out the rest of the innings on the bench—but not Cal. Instead, he was able to ignore the pain enough to finish with his teammates.

By toughing it out, Cal proved that he was just as tough mentally as he was physically. He later stated that if you want to be successful in anything in life, the first step is to "just show up." Whether he was in pain or feeling fine, that's what Cal Ripken Jr. did. In fact, he holds the record for the most consecutive games played in the MLB! He ended up playing 2,632 consecutive games over a 16-year period (all the way up to 1998), without ever once calling in sick! He ended his streak in 1998, and ultimately retired in 2001—but that really was quite a run!

Let that be a lesson to you the next time you're tempted to take a day off. The real overachievers keep at it!

FUN FACTS ABOUT CAL RIPKEN JR!

- His full name is Calvin Edwin Ripken Jr.
- He went to Aberdeen High School in Maryland.
- In the Minor Leagues, he played for the Bluefield Orioles.
- His entire Major League career was spent with the Baltimore Orioles.
- His last game for the MLB occurred on October 6th, 2001.

LEARN SOME CAL RIPKEN JR. TRIVIA!

What was Cal Ripken Jr.'s nickname?

Iron Man.

What was "The Streak?"

Cal Ripken Jr.'s record-breaking streak of consecutive games played.

When was Cal Ripken Jr. inducted into the Baseball Hall of Fame?

In 2007.

What's Cal's favorite food?

Seafood in general, and crabcakes in particular.

Where was he born?

Havre de Grace, Maryland.

REAL-LIFE LESSONS FROM CAL RIPKEN JR!

- Have good attendance!
- Stay humble.
- Keep a steady routine.
- Always try to improve.
- Stay positive.

I have included these free downloadable gifts to help light up your inner inspiration & reach your potential.

While you are reading through the stories, lessons and trivia, we recommend that you make use of all the bonuses we've attached here!

All our bonuses have been made specifically to help young athletes feel fired up, get inspired from the best to ever do it, and most importantly fall more in love with this incredible game!

Here's a list of what you're getting:

1) 250 Fun Facts From The World Of Sports
2) Sports Practice and Game Calendar
3) 5 Fun Exercise Drills for Kids
4) The BEST Advice From The Greatest Athletes Of All Time
5) The Mental Mindset Guided Meditation & Affirmation Collection
6) The Most Famous Events In Sports History And What They Can Teach Us

Now, it's over to you to scan the QR code, follow the instructions & get started!

SEAN BURROUGHS
THE COMEBACK KID

Sean Patrick Burroughs was born on September 12th, 1980, in Atlanta, Georgia. He is the son of Jeff Burroughs, who in his own heyday played for the Atlanta Braves. Considering his father's pedigree, it was almost a given that little Sean would grow up playing ball.

When he was a kid, his family moved from Georgia all the way over to Long Beach, California, where he played on the local Little League team. Sean made it all the way to the Little League World Series as a star pitcher, where he wowed crowds by throwing no hitters. He actually won championships in both 1992 and 1993, and was interviewed after one of these big wins. At one point, he was asked what he'd had for breakfast that morning. Sean stated that he had eaten "three big bowls of cereal." The kid really did eat his Wheaties that morning!

Sean was just a kid, but he was already a superstar. He attracted so much attention that he was invited on the David Letterman Show. David Letterman was a big-time, late-night TV host. He enjoyed joking and laughing with the young prodigy, while speculating over the big things that possibly awaited him in the future.

When Sean grew up, he was drafted into the big leagues, where he played for the San Diego Padres in 1998, right out of high school.

That year was a big one for baseball, with players such as Mark McGwire, Sammy Sosa, and Barry Bonds all coming out as power hitters with the potential to set the record for the home runs. It was in this home run derby that Sean Burroughs made his debut.

Always a quick learner, Sean excelled on the field and was named MVP by the 2000 season. He also earned a gold medal in the 2000 Olympics held in Sydney, Australia. He was rated as a top prospect in the MLB and maintained a vital role as the Padres' third baseman during the 2003 and 2004 seasons. The 2005 season wasn't his best, however, and he fell off track. The Padres began to question his abilities and ended up trading him to the Tampa Bay Rays.

Burroughs started playing for the Tampa Bay Rays in 2006, which proved to be his worst season on record. After his poor showing, he ended up getting bounced to an affiliate of Tampa Bay, the "Durham Bulls. This move didn't prove much better. Things continued to look grim, so he opted for early retirement in 2007. He was only 27 years old at the time.

For most people, retirement is a happy period of rest and relaxation after many years on the job. But for Sean, it felt like he had just dropped off the map and given up. It wasn't the happy ending he had hoped for, and he quickly became lost as to what to do with the rest of his life. He began living out of hotels, with no real direction. He soon became mixed up with drugs and alcohol, and found it hard to function. This was no way to live life!

Thankfully for Sean Burroughs, he was able to pull through this difficult period. After getting his act together, he decided he wanted to return to baseball. He trained hard and managed to get signed to the Minor Leagues by the Arizona Diamondbacks. This opened the door for a stint with the Minnesota Twins in 2012, and then the LA Dodgers in 2013, before he was shuffled over to the East Coast to play for Bridgeport Bluefish in 2014.

It certainly wasn't easy to make a comeback at this point. Besides having to get himself back into top shape, he had to face the economic hurdles of playing in the Minors. Minor League baseball is not known to pay very well, and most players have to find ways to minimize their expenses just to get by and be able to keep on playing.

For Sean, this meant having to become a boarder with a local family. It might sound like an odd relationship, but the family were known supporters of the team, and apparently boarded players frequently. According to Sean, he had to learn to be a proper house guest, abide by house rules, and mind his manners, all so he could stay focused on sharpening his game. But it didn't matter what it took—Sean Burroughs was back!

FUN FACTS ABOUT SEAN BURROUGHS!

- He was a breakout Little League star.
- He appeared on David Letterman.
- He was named MVP in 2000.
- He earned a gold medal at the 2000 Olympics.
- His dad, Jeff Burroughs, is a former MLB player.

LEARN SOME SEAN BURROUGHS TRIVIA!

Where did Sean go for the Olympics?

He played in the 2000 Olympics, which was hosted in Sydney, Australia.

When did Sean first retire?

He first retired in 2007, before later mounting a comeback.

What batting ritual did Sean have?

He used to hit home plate six times with his bat before getting ready to swing.

What's his favorite food?

He's been known to dine on a good dish of spaghetti and meatballs.

What's his nickname?

Sausage, or just Sauce for short (this nickname can apparently be traced all the way back to his Little League days!).

REAL-LIFE LESSONS
FROM SEAN BURROUGHS!

- Pick yourself up when you fall.
- Overcome adversity.
- Maintain a positive attitude.
- Make the best of everything.
- Don't dwell on the past.

ICHIR
51

ICHIRO SUZUKI DO WHAT IT TAKES TO BREAK OUT OF THE MOLD!

Ichiro Suzuki was born in Japan on October 22nd, 1973. Baseball had been popular for quite some time in Japan, and during the Second World War, which saw a prolonged US presence in the region, American service members made the game even more popular. New baseball stadiums were built, and love of the game was widely encouraged.

Ichiro Suzuki was one of those who grew up loving baseball. He grew up near the city of Nagoya, which was known for their hometown team called the Chunichi Dragons. His dad was a big-time fan, and involved his son in the sport as soon as he was old enough to catch. Ichiro was gifted with a baseball mitt when he was just 3 years old!

Ichiro fondly remembers that moment, recalling that this was no kid's glove, but rather a real, regular issue baseball glove. It might have been a bit big for his hand, but he grew into it soon enough. Ichiro and his baseball mitt were inseparable, and he was soon playing for the very Little League team that his father coached.

Ichiro's whole family soon became involved in the effort. He had a special exercise routine and a tailor-made diet. He later recalled that an aunt would serve him a specially made protein boosting soup. By the time Ichiro was in the fifth grade, he was able to hit pitches coming at him at more than 60 miles an hour.

We know this because Ichiro and his dad would go to a batting center and hit pitches set to this speed. People who knew the youngster couldn't believe what they were seeing, but Ichiro and his father quietly kept at it. It was also his dad who is credited with advising Ichiro to watch other players, see what they were doing right, and then incorporate their winning style into his own routine.

Ichiro was a quick study. After seeing one game of the local Yomiuri Giants and watching their star hitter launch the ball practically into orbit, he went home and imitated that hitter's stance. He saw that the hitter would end up on one leg as he swung, with his other leg swinging back and forth like a pendulum in order to maintain the perfect balance.

Ichiro was a force to be reckoned with by the time he played for the team at his junior high school. He was regularly hitting 80-mile-an-hour pitches, and there seemed to be no stopping him.

Ichiro enrolled at Aiko Dai Meiden High School, which had a formidable baseball team at the time. In fact, 11 former players had already made it to the pros in Japan. Ichiro was thrilled to go to the school and join the team. The school was a bit far from his home, however, and this meant that Ichiro had to stay in a special dorm. He knew that he would be a bit homesick, but he was living his dream, so he didn't hesitate to go for it.

Life in the dorm wasn't easy, since the upperclassmen set a bunch of harsh, arbitrary rules that they expected the newbies to follow. Japan is known for having rather rigid protocols when it comes to respecting one's elders, and the freshmen were expected to respect their elder classmates! Ichiro was even forced to cook rice for the older students. If he failed to do so, he was sure to hear about it later!

On one occasion he was made to cook rice for the older students in the dorm, and accidentally burnt some of it. To show their displeasure, the upperclassmen punished him by ordering him to kneel on the lid of a garbage can while he reflected upon his mistakes.

The adversity and harsh treatment he faced only made Ichiro a tougher, more formidable player. And since he couldn't refuse his orders from the upperclassman, which took up his practice time, Ichiro decided to sacrifice sleep. He knew that if he slept less, he could get more done, so he began getting up at 3:00 in the morning to get a jump on his assigned dorm duties.

While this routine might have worked for Ichiro, it's definitely not for everyone. Most of us need at least 8 hours of sleep per night, and should try and make sure that we get it most of the time.

Ichiro kept working as hard as he could, and by his sophomore year, his team had made it to a regional tournament. He continued to make a name for himself in the coming years, and after high school, he managed to get drafted as an outfielder for a team called the Orix Blue Wave.

Ichiro had made the big leagues. His father had hoped that he would join the local legends, the Chunichi Dragons, but Ichiro was happy just to be on a professional team. It wasn't going to be easy however, since many of his teammates were older, more experienced, and bigger! Ichiro was a small guy, short and skinny. As such, he was immediately advised to bulk up. It was time for more of his auntie's protein soup!

In addition to eating protein soup, he started an even more vigorous workout routine. He did well, and by July he was called up to the Major League division of the Orix Blue Wave.

Unfortunately. He was soon bounced back down to the Minor Leagues. He was told he needed more experience. He tried his best, and was soon back into the Majors, but it wasn't long before he was demoted to the Minors once again! He shifted back and forth a few more times before he was finally deemed good enough to remain in the Major Leagues.

One of Ichiro's best seasons came in 1993, when he began to break out as a home run hitter. But his manager, Shozo Doi, didn't like Ichiro's style and began to accuse him of "showing off" too much. The two developed a fraught relationship, and the fact that his boss had taken a distinct dislike to him gave Ichiro a lot of problems. Nevertheless, Ichiro persevered, and as the 1993 season came to a close, he had the opportunity to take part in a special "winter league" over in the American state of Hawaii.

This was an international effort, which showcased some of the best Japanese players, as well as some American players. Ichiro loved the diversity of this team, not only because his teammates hailed from many different parts of the world, but because they all had very unique approaches to baseball, just like him. As much as his coach back home wanted him to conform to what he thought was the "proper" way to play, in Hawaii, Ichiro found a much more accepting environment for his unique approach to the game.

Everything seemed to be falling into place for Ichiro. Upon his return to Japan, he was surprised to learn that his old manager had been replaced by a new one—Akira Ogi. Normally, this might be cause for alarm, since no one knows what changes new management might bring. But, soon enough, Ichiro realized that it was cause for celebration.

Ichiro had already met Ogi during his stint in Hawaii, and had found him to be an agreeable person to work with. Ogi was much more open-minded, and was open to Ichiro's unique style and approach. In fact, he was ready to nurture and refine the methodology that Ichiro had developed. Ichiro went into the 1994 season with a full head of steam. He hit four home runs and had a high batting average. By mid-season, the Orix Blue Wave were close to winning the Pacific League Pennant.

Unfortunately, they were soundly defeated by another rising team, the Seibu Lions. Nevertheless, Ichiro's performance was so outstanding that many began to speak of him possibly shifting over to the big leagues in America. As much as the Japanese loved their baseball, they knew that there was more opportunity for a player who was recruited into the Major Leagues.

During all of this speculation,, the Japanese city of Kobe was struck by a terrible earthquake and thousands of people died. Ichiro felt terrible and wanted to do something to help. In order to show their solidarity, he and his teammates played the 1995 season with special uniforms, with the phrase, "Gamarou Kobe" emblazoned on the sleeves. The phrase translates as "Let's Do Our Best for Kobe!"

Ichiro meant it. He played his heart out that year, putting on an especially inspired performance when facing a tough team called the Chiba Lotte Marines. In this game, he faced off against a tough pitcher by the name of Hideki Irabu. Hideki was good, but Ichiro was better. All of those years of swinging at fast balls in batting cages paid off, with Ichiro cracking his bat into the best pitches Hideki could throw.

The next major change in his life occurred in late 1998, when Ichiro was chosen to train with the Seattle Mariners. He arrived at the Mariners training camp, which was based out of Arizona at the time, in February of 1999. Ichiro held American baseball in the highest esteem, and openly wondered if he had what it took to play in the American big leagues. Ichiro—along with the rest of the world—was about to find out.

Ichiro's performance and unique style attracted major interest, and by the time he went back to Japan, he knew that he had what it took to thrive in the US. He spent the next couple of seasons perfecting his skills in Japan, but his heart was in America!

During the 2001 season, his dreams came true: He was drafted by the Seattle Mariners. The contract was a lucrative one, with the Mariners paying over $13 million to the Blue Wave just for the deal, along with the $15 million promised to Ichiro himself.

Ichiro joined the Mariners as a right fielder. On April 6th, 2001, he hit his first home run playing for a US Major League baseball team. Soon, fans in the stand were literally shouting his name. They had never seen a player who played quite like Ichiro.

Even though he was chided by previous managers in Japan and told to conform and not stand out, Ichiro's unique skill and talent ended up making major waves. So, the next time someone tells you to keep your head down and mind the status quo, think of Ichiro and don't hesitate to break the mold!

FUN FACTS ABOUT ICHIRO SUZUKI!

- Growing up, he strengthened his arms by hitting wiffle balls with a heavy shovel.
- Many considered him to be too small for baseball.
- His old manager back in Japan, Shozo Doi, criticized his unorthodox swing.
- In 1994, he broke records for the Pacific League with his batting average.
- He began playing for the Seattle Mariners in 2001.

LEARN SOME ICHIRO SUZUKI TRIVIA!

What hand does Ichiro bat with?

Ichiro typically bats with his left hand, although he is known as a "switch hitter," meaning he can switch and hit with his other hand if necessary.

What was Ichiro's first season in MLB?

He made his debut in the 2001 season.

What three awards did Ichiro win as a rookie?

He won Rookie of the Year and MVP, as well as the American League batting title.

What are Ichiro's favorite foods?

Hot dogs, pizza, and sushi.

If he was a superhero, what superpower would he want?

Ichiro was once asked this question in an interview. He stated that he would like to be invisible.

REAL-LIFE LESSONS FROM ICHIRO SUZUKI

- Don't let judgmental people bring you down.
- Follow your own convictions.
- Find your sweet spot when it comes to training and stick to it.
- Be creative.
- Have fun.

THE LITTLE-KNOWN MARVEL OF WILLIE STARGELL

Willie Stargell was a phenomenon. For most people, such praise might be mere hyperbole, but for Stargell it was the truth. Willie was born on March 6th, 1940, in the town of Earlsboro, Oklahoma. His upbringing wasn't easy, and after his parents' marriage ended in divorce, he left his broken home to live with one of his aunts in Florida.

It took some time for his parents to get their heads straight, but soon his mom was asking about him and he ended up moving in with her in Alameda, California. He enrolled at Encinal High School, where he perfected his throwing arm on the high school team.

Willie later recalled that many of his teammates were simply local kids in the neighborhood. He was friendly with all of them, and the team was almost like a big extended family. Two of his teammates—Curt Motton and Tommy Harper—later went on to the big leagues.

Willie's athletic devotion was initially split between football and baseball, but after he ended up on the wrong end of a particularly brutal tackle that left him with a busted knee, he decided that football might not be for him, after all.

From this point forward, he put all of his energy in baseball. The hard work paid off, and the recruiters soon took notice. He was eventually drafted by the Pittsburgh Pirates. He spent some time in training with the farm teams before he was able to make his way to the big leagues. He had a lot of adversity to work through. Not only did he need to perfect his game, he also had to deal with prejudice.

Baseball has long been racially integrated, but in the late 1950s and early 1960s, when Willie was rising to prominence, there was still a lot of animosity in many parts of the United States when it came to having African American players on the same teams as Caucasians. This was especially true in southern parts of the United States, which had a long history of segregation.

Willie Stargell had grown up in a fairly inclusive environment, and was shocked to find that some folks disliked him for no other reason than the color of his skin. Nevertheless, with the encouragement of his friends, family, and fellow teammates, he was able to persevere and ignore any taunts thrown his way.

Rather than give up, he just trained harder. His hard work paid off, and as the 1961 season came to a close, Willie was notified by the Pirates that they wanted to sign him to the big leagues.

He played his first official MLB game for the Pirates in 1962, when he was 22 years old. It was a great debut for a newbie, but the following season wasn't his best. He made up for it in 1964 by literally hitting the ball out of the park. He hit a tremendous home run when the Pirates played at Shea Stadium that made the crowd go wild.

Willie's home life had been going through tremendous changes. He had gotten married to his high school sweetheart, with whom he had two kids, but the union ended in divorce. Willie then remarried a woman named Dolores, with whom he had a son. He would later joke that the fact that Dolores was a good cook was the reason for his rapid weight gain.

Willie had previously been skinny, but was now becoming increasingly hefty. This might have been beneficial for football, but carrying around extra pounds when trying to run to second base was not considered an asset! He was soon put on a strict diet and worked hard to shed the pounds.

The rest of the 1960s saw Stargell head into another slump, but the 1969 season ended up being one of his best. That kickstarted an entire decade in which Willie dominated the field.

By September of 1970, Willie and the team had successfully won the Eastern Division Title. This brought them within striking distance of the upcoming World Series. Unfortunately, they were ultimately outdone by the Cincinnati Reds, and failed to make it to the World Series. They continued persevering, however, and in 1971 they not only made it to the World Series, *they won.*

Willie was a star player, but he emphasized teamwork and had the team use the hit song "We are Family" as their opening theme. He also encouraged his teammates by passing out "stars" in recognition of good plays, which were dubbed "Stargell Stars."

Willie Stargell was sending a clear message—his teammates were his family and he thought the world of them. He wasn't going to let them down, and he didn't expect them to let him down either. The Pirates kept at it, and managed to win the World Series again in 1979, when Willie, who was affectionately known as Pops, was 39 years old. Willie retired a happy man a few years later in 1982, at the age of 42.

FUN FACTS ABOUT WILLIE STARGELL!

- His MLB career officially began in 1962/
- He was inducted into the Hall of Fame in 1988.
- He scored a total of 475 homers for the Pittsburgh Pirates.
- Pirates players are given the "Stargell Star" for good plays.
- Stargell was a two-time World Series champ.

LEARN SOME WILLIE STARGELL TRIVIA!

What number was on Willie Stargell's jersey?

He wore number 8!

How many World Series wins does Willie Stargell have?

Two: 1971 and 1979.

What was his nickname?

Pops!

What was his favorite food?

Fried chicken!

What was his batting hand?

Willie Stargell was a left-handed batter.

REAL-LIFE LESSONS FROM WILLIE STARGELL!

- Persevere.
- Encourage others.
- Do your best.
- Stay positive.
- Keep focused.

RED SOX

PLAY IT LIKE YOU MEAN IT
PEDRO MARTINEZ

Pedro Martinez was born on October 25th, 1971, in the village of Mano Guayabo, on the Caribbean island nation of the Dominican Republic. He grew up on a farm with his brothers and sisters, where his parents grew their own food. His father, Paulino, also worked as a janitor in order to bring in some extra money for the family. As a kid, Pedro helped out on the farm and around the house as much as he could, but in his free time he was eager to play ball.

Playing baseball was a different experience in his poor village than it was in many other parts of the world, since Pedro often didn't have the proper equipment. There were times when he lacked even a proper bat and ball. He and his buddies often substituted a broom for a bat, and used rolled-up socks, fruit, and even rocks as their baseballs.

It wasn't always pretty whacking socks with a broom, but it served as practice all the same. And Pedro practiced a lot. He practiced in the fields and he practiced in the middle of the street.

Pedro was an active kid and stayed away from home a lot. Partly this was to burn up his high amounts of energy, but he likely also did so to stay away from the growing problems in his household. His parents' marriage came to an end when he was just nine years old. This abrupt split was devastating for Pedro, but fortunately his big brother Ramon helped fill the gap and did what he could to aid his little brother in learning baseball and everything else that was important in life.

Ramon himself was a great baseball player, and was eventually drafted by the Minor League team called the Santo Domingo Dodgers in the Dominican Republic. Pedro would often follow his brother to practice. He acted as a kind of unofficial assistant, carrying Ramon's gear to the baseball field. He also continued to practice his own skills on the sidelines.

One day, while he was engaged in his typical warmup routine, a coach happened to observe him. After watching Pedro, the coach said he believed the young athlete had what it took to play on an official team, just like Ramon.

Shortly thereafter, Ramon got his ticket to the big leagues and left for the US, where he eventually ended up playing for the LA Dodgers. Pedro soon followed in his brother's footsteps. Like his brother, Pedro was approached at the age of 16 by a recruiter who wanted him to train as a potential prospect for the Dodgers.

Pedro trained in Santo Domingo while he finished up the rest of his schooling. Then, in 1990, the Dodgers sent Pedro off to Great Falls, Montana, so that he could pitch on a rookie team there. He was a phenomenal pitcher right out of the gate, striking out 82 batters during the course of the season.

In 1991, Pedro was put on the Class A team, based in Bakersfield, California.

He did exceedingly well, and was bumped up to the next level, playing on a Class AA team in San Antonio, Texas. This frequent shifting and moving around while working their way up the ladder can be exhausting for players. Fortunately for Pedro, his brother Ramon had been through it all before and was there to encourage him not to lose hope. He told him it was all part of the process of moving on to better things.

Although Pedro's teams lost many games, he stood out as a talented player. It didn't take long for the Dodgers to bump Pedro up again, this time to a Class AAA team. He was placed on the Albuquerque Dukes, where he finished up the 1991 season. Then, in 1992, Pedro finally made it into the Majors, where he was placed on the official roster of the LA Dodgers.

His big debut came as a relief pitcher during a game against the Cincinnati Reds on September 24th, 1992. After the season came to a close, he and his brother Ramon headed back to the Dominican Republic to visit family and friends and enjoy some well-deserved rest. As soon as the 1993 season began, however, Pedro returned stateside in order to begin spring training.

He arrived at the Dodgers training camp in Florida in early 1993. But Pedro was soon disappointed to learn that he was going to be sent back to the minors in Albuquerque for some additional training. He was good, but management thought he could be better. Pedro was devastated, but his brother reassured him that this was likely just a small setback. With enough training, he would be right back in the big leagues in no time.

Ramon was right. Before the season was over, Pedro was back with the Dodgers. He even had the pleasure of relieving his own brother Ramon when the Dodgers faced off against the Atlanta Braves. Changes were on the way, however, and Pedro was traded to the Montreal Expos in 1994. He was dismayed to leave the team that his brother was on, but he was even more determined to succeed. No matter what hand he was dealt, he was determined to make the best of it.

With the Expos, he worked harder than ever and became known as a formidable pitcher. During one infamous game that season, he almost managed to pitch a perfect game. This means that Pedro almost pitched a game that had no hits or walks—nothing but struck-out batters! The game wasn't infamous due to his near perfection, however. Instead, it was due to the reaction of one of the players on the opposing team.

The Montreal Expos were playing against the Cincinnati Reds, and Pedro sent a fast ball flying toward Reds batter Reggie Sanders. Reggie wasn't able to hit the fast pitch, and the ball ended up hitting him on the elbow. Pedro would later swear that this was not intentional, but Sanders apparently thought it was. Maybe he was frustrated that he and the rest of his team couldn't hit any of the balls Pedro threw!

At any rate, getting hit in the elbow by Pedro was apparently the last straw for Reggie. He suddenly threw his bat down and ran straight for Pedro! Pedro was tackled by the mad batter right there on the pitcher's mound. Soon, several other players joined in, and a riot broke out on the field.

The umpire sought to regain control and eventually managed to break up the fight. The game then resumed, and Pedro won it for the Montreal Expos. His reputation had taken a hit, however, and it was soon whispered that perhaps he did try to hit batters on purpose. Pedro knew the truth—he knew that it wasn't his fault if batters couldn't hit his pitches. He wasn't going to take the blame for that. Pedro ignored his critics and kept perfecting his aim.

In 1997, he was drafted by the Boston Red Sox. Pedro was becoming an in-demand pitcher just when many teams needed them badly, for the late 1990s was the time when all-star sluggers such as Mark McGwire, Sammy Sosa, Ken Griffey Jr., and Barry Bonds were hitting record numbers of home runs.

But even these heavy hitters had a hard time when the ball was being pitched by Pedro. The 1998 season saw Pedro at his height of perfection, with him pitching a nearly perfect game against Oakland, in which not a single batter from the opposing team got a hit until the fourth inning. Pedro struck out 11 different batters across seven innings, and the Red Sox triumphed over Oakland with a 2-0 win.

Many people openly wondered about the team's chances in the World Series, but the Red Sox were ultimately stopped by the Cleveland Indians, who were in turn knocked out of the running by the New York Yankees. The Yankees famously went on to win the World Series that year. Even so, it was a great year for the Red Sox, and an even better one for Pedro Martinez. And there was more to come. In 1999, Pedro was named MVP for the Boston Red Sox.

Over the next few years, the team did okay, but always seemed to fall short in the playoffs. It wasn't until the 2004 season that they truly rose to the occasion. That year, Pedro helped lead the Boston Red Sox all the way to the World Series—and this time, they won. Baseball fans can be a superstitious lot, and there had long been whispers that the Red Sox were under some sort of curse. How else could one explain the fact that they had not won a World Series since 1918? But Pedro, along with skilled teammates such as David Ortiz (famously known as Big Papi?) helped the Red Sox break this curse and reclaim the title.

After helping Boston win the World Series, Pedro Martinez became a free agent and played with a couple of other teams (including the New York Mets and Philadelphia Phillies) before his official retirement in 2011. But at the end of his career, Pedro Martinez was best known in Boston as the guy who lifted Bambino's curse!

This was important for Boston Red Sox fans, who believed their team had been cursed ever since the day former Red Sox player Babe Ruth (aka the Great Bambino) was traded to the New York Yankees in 1919. After Babe left, Boston didn't win another World Series until that fateful 2004 season.

FUN FACTS ABOUT PEDRO MARTINEZ!

- Red Sox Fans say he helped lift the Curse of the Bambino.
- Pedro was one of the best pitchers in the league.
- In 1994, one of Pedro's pitches sparked a brawl.
- He played a part in bringing David Ortiz to the Red Sox.
- He retired in 2011.

LEARN SOME PEDRO MARTINEZ TRIVIA!

Who tackled Pedro at the pitcher's mound, sparking a baseball brawl?

Reggie Sanders.

What team did Pedro play for after leaving the Boston Red Sox?

He played for the New York Mets from 2005 to 2008.

When was Pedro tied to a pole?

Pedro was known to be a chatterbox. In 1999, his teammates tired of his incessant banter in the dugout, tied him to a pole, and joked that they would leave him there!

What is his nickname?

El Grande.

What are his favorite movies?

Shrek, Titanic, and The Passion of the Christ.

REAL-LIFE LESSONS FROM PEDRO MARTINEZ!

- Don't take life too seriously.
- Practice makes perfect.
- Help others.
- Keep an open mind.
- Pace yourself.

IT'S JUST MIGGY BEING MIGGY
MIGUEL CABRERA

Miguel Cabrera and his quest for the "Triple Crown" is legendary. In baseball, the Triple Crown is a special distinction given to a batter who manages to earn three batting honors in a season. They have to take top honors in RBIs, home runs, and overall batting average. It's a rare feat, and Miguel's journey to the crown is legendary.

Miguel was born on April 18th, 1983, in the South American nation of Venezuela. He grew up in a tiny house that consisted of a kitchen, a bathroom, and two bedrooms. He lived in this tiny home with his family, crowded together with not much more than their love for each other. They didn't have a lot of money. In fact, when Miguel caught the baseball bug, he didn't even have a real baseball or bat to play with. He made his first forays into baseball with nothing more than a hefty stick and wadded-up piece of paper. This is not exactly MLB-certified equipment, but for the young boy growing up in Venezuela, it would have to make do.

Miguel—or Miggy, as his family liked to call him—was nevertheless a happy kid who always tried his best. He never wanted to let his family down, and he especially wanted to impress his father, whom he loved and looked up to. His dad had actually played ball himself in his youth, even though he eventually gave up the sport to become a mechanic. When Miguel picked up his bat (or stick), in many ways, he was trying to live the dream that his father had given up to support his family.

Interestingly, his father was not the only family member who played ball. Miguel's mother had also spent some time on a local Venezuelan team. He was just a baby hanging out in the dugout when his mom played shortstop on a Venezuelan field. To say that baseball was a family tradition for the Cabrera family is an understatement, so it's really no surprise that Miguel picked up the bat at such an early age.

Miguel was only 4 years old when he began to really give baseball some serious thought. This early adoption of the sport was beneficial for Miguel's athletic ability.

By the time he was 14, Miguel had begun to tower over his peers when it came to skill on the baseball diamond.

His family knew that he was talented, but they also instilled in him the importance of taking slow and measured steps toward his dream. He was still in his teens, and he had some growing up to do. His parents didn't want anyone to take advantage of him. They encouraged him to take it easy and not rush into anything. Along with playing ball, they wanted him to live a normal teenage life and finish school.

When Miguel was 14, he was placed in a special "baseball school" in Cagua, Venezuela. This school emphasized baseball and developed the talents of young players, but at the same time made sure that young prospects such as Miguel stayed grounded and received a normal education. He was able to work on improving his batting average while learning how to add, subtract, and multiply.

In the meantime, scouts from the US began to take notice of Miguel's efforts. Soon, special reps from teams like the Minnesota Twins, New York Yankees, and LA Dodgers were on the scene to check him out. They knew a budding talent when they saw one, and neither of these baseball organizations wanted to miss out on a powerful future prospect.

As much as these teams were interested in Miggy, he already had an interest of his own. He had heard a lot of good things about the Florida Marlins, who had won the 1997 World Series. Florida isn't that far from Latin America, and has an especially strong pull for many Latino players. Many of Miguel's own personal heroes, such as Alex Gonzalez, Livian Hernandez, and Edgar Renteria, already played for the Marlins. It was likely this sense of familiarity that encouraged Miguel to look towards Florida for his future.

The door opened for Miguel on July 2nd, 1999, when the 16-year-old was given a $1.8 million contract to sign with the Florida Marlins. Some of the other teams that had been looking into Miggy were actually pretty frustrated that the Marlins beat them to the punch. Yankees owner George Steinbrenner is said to have been so angry that they missed out on recruiting Miguel that he dismissed three of his own scouts.

At any rate, Miguel was quite happy with the arrangement, and he was ready to fly to Florida to begin his journey to the Major Leagues. But although he had the Majors in his sights, he first had to get through the Minor League system.

By the time he turned 17 in 2000 Miguel was playing for a Gulf Coast Minor League team that was directly affiliated with the Florida Marlins. This team was based out of suburban Jupiter, Florida, not far from Miami. It was here, in Jupiter's Dean Stadium, that Miguel further perfected his craft.

Although he was later known as a big hitter, home runs were pretty rare when Miguel was young. Even so, he was reliable, with a steady and respectable batting average. Rather than hitting homers, his specialty at this time was hitting doubles and triples.

When not at bat, Miggy was also an excellent fielder who was especially skilled at the utilitarian position of shortstop.

He was good at stopping balls, and was able to quickly throw the ball where it needed to go. Perhaps all of those days watching his mom play the same position paid off. Whatever the case, Miggy played well enough that he was bumped up to the Kane County Cougars, which was a Class A Minor League team affiliated with the Marlins at the time.

This was a move up, but it meant that Miguel Cabrera would have to leave his sunny stomping grounds of Florida for Chicago, Illinois, where the Cougars were based. Such a transition would be daunting for anyone, especially for someone like Miguel, who had never even seen snow! Nevertheless, Miggy didn't hesitate, since he knew that his dreams were on the line. He was dedicated to doing well in baseball, and if he had to face the chilly winds of the Windy City of Chicago to make it big, then so be it.

Miggy held onto that fierce determination during his entire journey through the Minors and into the big leagues. His hard work paid off when he was officially recruited to the main Florida Marlins Major League team in 2003. He was still fairly young at just 20 years old when he first stepped onto the field on June 20th, 2003, when the Marlins faced off against their in-state rivals, the Tampa Bay Devil Rays.

Miggy's first game with the Marlins was a bit of a disappointment. He stumbled and made mistakes that he didn't normally make. Fortunately, the management at the Marlins did what they could to mentor Miggy and get his mind in shape. No matter how strong you are physically, if your head's not straight, your game will suffer. Miggy learned that the hard way his opening night, but that made him decide he just needed to try harder By July, he had improved his game so much that he was named National League Rookie of the Month.

Miguel continued to perform well from this point forward, and he and his team went on to win the World Series, beating the New York Yankees. It's always thrilling for a ballplayer to be on a team that wins the World Series, but it must have been especially exciting for Miggy, since this was only his first year in the Majors!

Miggy knew that the win wasn't due to just him, but to solid teamwork between him and the other players on his team. He knew the value of teamwork, and so should the rest of us. Whether in baseball or in life in general, it takes more than one member of a team to get the job done.

Miguel stayed with the Marlins for another few years before being traded to the Detroit Tigers. He was now an older and more experienced player, and he worked hard to further hone his abilities. While with the Tigers, he became one of the most consistent players in the league, ultimately resulting in him winning the Triple Crown in 2012.

Miguel has since become a mentor, founding the Miguel Cabrera Foundation. This foundation focuses on teaching youngsters how they can excel and reach their goals. He worked hard and made his dreams come true. If you work hard like him, the same can happen for you.

FUN FACTS ABOUT MIGUEL CABRERA!

- Miguel is originally from Venezuela.
- He was signed by the Marlins in 1999.
- He's a 12-time MLB All-Star.
- He played for the Detroit Tigers from 2008 to 2023.
- Miguel Cabrera retired in 2023.

LEARN SOME MIGUEL CABRERA TRIVIA!

His mom played ball.

Yes, it's true! In her heyday, Miggy's mom was a star on a Venezuelan national softball team.

What's his favorite vacation spot?

Disney World! Miggy has been a Disney fanatic ever since he was a kid.

Is Miguel a recording artist?

Yes! He has been featured on a hip hop song called "Miggy at Bat."

How many World Series rings does he have?

One.

What is his nickname?

Miggy, of course!

REAL-LIFE LESSONS FROM MIGUEL CABRERA!

- Have passion for what you do.
- Be dedicated.
- Be a team player.
- Have fun.
- Appreciate your fanbase.

ALBERT PUJOLS
HOW HE BECAME MOST VALUABLE PLAYER

Albert Pujols was one of the most efficient players in the league. In fact, he performed so well he was called a baseball "machine." He was always running on all cylinders, and had a fantastic run while he was with the MLB.

Albert was born on January 16th, 1980, in Santo Domingo, Dominican Republic. He grew up playing ball, and dreamt of playing in the big leagues. His story of growing up in the Dominican Republic is similar to many other players from the region. He would later reflect that he never had much in the way of proper equipment, and often used nothing more than a stick to hit whatever item happened to look like a baseball.

As he grew older, his family immigrated to the United States in search of a better life. Albert brought his love of baseball with him. He played ball for Fort Osage High School in Missouri. He played shortstop and led his team to the championships in 1997. Shortly thereafter, he was given a college scholarship to play ball for Maple Woods Community College.

It wasn't long before Major League Baseball came calling. As is typically the case, however, he first had to do a brief stint in the Minor League farm system. In 2000, he played on a team called the Peoria Chiefs located in Peoria, Illinois. He was a hard and diligent worker on the Chiefs, and it didn't take long for him to get bumped up to Triple-A status and placed on the top farm team, the Memphis Redbirds. There, he showed true promise with a high batting average and great stats across the board.

It was clear he was ready for the Majors, and he was placed on the regular St. Louis Cardinals team in 2001. This was a transitional year for the Cardinals, for their top player, Mark McGwire, was getting ready to retire. Mark was famous for his record-breaking home runs in the late 1990s, but by 2001 he was worn out and slowing down.

Albert Pujols was looked upon as the next-generation player who would be tasked with picking up the slack. He hit the ground running, gaining 100 RBIs during the course of his first five seasons on the team. He later attributed his solid debut to hard work and being a real team player.

Albert Pujols later remarked that he was just focused on doing his part to ensure that the Cardinals would win, and it was his efforts to help the team that boosted his own personal stats. As he put it at the time, "I want to win. The numbers are going to be there if you help your team win. If you play the game the right way. Move the guy over. Steal a base. Make some plays. That's when your numbers are going to be there."

That meant he had to work hard. His regular fitness regimen included some pretty serious weight lifting aimed at bulking up the muscles in his forearms. This extra bit of forearm strength is vital for any batter hoping to blast one out of the park

Albert Pujols kept up this tremendous work ethic, and in the 2002 season his stats were once again off the charts. The next season was even better, and by 2004 he was the clear MVP of the Cardinals as they went head-to-head against the Houston Astros in a heated contest for the National League title.

During one game with the Astros, Albert hit a home run in the very first inning. He then launched another homer in the second matchup, which helped to ensure that the Cardinals stayed in the lead. Game 4 saw another home run, as did Game 6. The Cardinals ultimately won the National League title and went on to face the Boston Red Sox in the World Series.

They didn't fare as well against the Sox, and fell short of victory during the World Series. Nevertheless, it was quite a ride, and the team had plenty to be proud of along the way. Albert's efforts were recognized by the upper management of the Cardinals, and he was rewarded with a new seven-year contract worth $100 million.

Albert left the Cardinals in 2012 to play for some other teams, but he never forgot the team that gave him his big break. Just before his retirement, he returned to the Cardinals in 2022 to play his last season of baseball. Albert never forgot where he started, and in the end his sense of class and loyalty showed through as he gave back to Cardinals fans what they had given to him.

FUN FACTS ABOUT ALBERT PUJOLS!

- He was born in 1980.
- His family moved to the US in 1996.
- His high school won a state championship in 1997.
- His first season in the big leagues was 2001.
- Albert established the Pujols Family Foundation in 2005.

LEARN SOME ALBERT PUJOLS TRIVIA!

What's the most impressive thing about Pujols' stats?

His consistency.

How many World Series wins does he have?

Two!

Who did Albert hit a home run off of during the Cardinals' 2001 home opener?

Colorado Rockies pitcher Denny Neagle.

What award has Albert Pujols won six times?

The Silver Slugger Award.

What is his nickname?

The Machine.

REAL-LIFE LESSONS FROM ALBERT PUJOLS!

- Be a leader.
- Be disciplined.
- Be consistent.
- Have a strong work ethic.
- Give back to the community.

WHEN IN DOUBT, YOU CAN DEPEND ON MIKE TROUT!

Mike Trout was born on August 7th, 1991, to his proud parents, Jeff and Debbie Trout. Born in Vineland, New Jersey, but brought up in Millville, Mike learned about baseball from an early age. This was due in large part to the fact that his dad played for the University of Delaware before heading into the Minor League farm system of the Minnesota Twins in the early 1980s.

Jeff sustained a bad injury to his knee and had to call it quits, but his boy with a love of the game, and Mike became an avid follower of the Philadelphia Phillies. He even went so far as to attend the Philadelphia Phillies parade after they won the World Series in 2008.

Mike Trout became quite a ballplayer himself, playing Little League and all throughout middle school and high school, where his team made the playoffs. Mike was a great baseball player, but he was also quite skilled at football and basketball. He graduated from high school in 2009 and fully anticipated playing ball in college, but the MLB Draft intervened.

Mike was deemed good enough to start in the farm system, and he didn't voice any complaints. He accepted a draft offer and was soon playing with a Minor League outfit called the Arizona Angels. He played well for the Angels, then finished off the season for the Cedar Rapids Kernels, which was a Class A Midwest League team at the time.

Just prior to the start of the 2010 season, Mike was listed as the "third-best prospect," according to Baseball America. Baseball America also considered him 85th best baseball player overall. He eventually went to the Rancho Cucamonga Quakes, which were a Class A Advanced California League. He did so well during the 2010 season that he was awarded with the Topps Minor League Player of the Year Award.

He then kicked off the 2011 season by playing with another Minor League team—the Arkansas Travelers. Mike's hard work paid off, and in the summer of 2011 he made his way to the big leagues, joining the Los Angeles Angels. His first season was a bit rocky, however, and he was sent back to the Minors for more practice.

Within a month, he'd been brought back to the Los Angeles Angels. Mike waltzed into Angel Stadium with the determination of a gladiator in the Roman Coliseum. He had taken a beating, and he knew it was now or never. He had to succeed, or risk being tossed out and thrown to the lions—or in his case, the Minors. He didn't disappoint. In his first game back with the Los Angeles Angels, he managed to hit a couple of homers right out the gate.

It was clear to all that Mike Trout was ready to play ball. Even so, his journey through the Minor League farm system was not yet over. Soon, he was sent back to finish the season with the Travelers. Then, during the 2012 season, he played for another Minor League team called the Salt Lake Bees. By April, he was brought back to the Angels, and by July, he was playing in the All Star Game.

The season that followed was incredible for Mike. He managed to hit a total of 30 home runs, score 125 runs, and steal 45 bases! He kept it up during the 2013 season, as well, at one point wowing fans by managing to hit a grand slam. This means that the bases were loaded (first, second, and third were all occupied) when he hit a home run. This is a big play, because it allows four different players to score, one after the other. He also played in the All Star Game that year. As the name implies, the All Star Game is a baseball exhibition game consisting of an assortment of all star players from all across the Major Leagues.

Mike repeated the feat in 2014, not only playing in the All Star Game, but also taking home the title of MVP. His greatest thrill, however, was playing alongside one of his idol's in the All Star Game—Derek Jeter.

Mike had always looked up to Jeter, and playing with him was a dream come true. Mike was 22 at the time, and Derek was 40. There was something very special about this moment in baseball history, which saw the older baseball legend passing off the torch to the next generation of greatness.

All in all, things were looking good for Mike Trout. Along with playing in the All Star game with Jeter, he also managed to tie the knot, getting married in 2014. Mike made the All Stars again in 2015, and incredibly was once again named MVP. Then his young family welcomed a new addition, with Mike's son making his grand debut on July 30th, 2020.

Today, Mike Trout is as content as a fish and happy as a clam! In fact, it could be said that Mike Trout has made happiness and fulfillment the centerpiece of his life.

We tend to make things more complicated than they have to be, but Mike shows us that a winning strategy in life is really pretty simple. Just do what makes you happy and everything else will follow.

FUN FACTS ABOUT MIKE TROUT!

- His old high school named their baseball field after him.
- Outside of Mike's hometown of Millville, a sign declares the town to be "Home of Mike Trout."
- He loves all things weather-related, and would like to be a TV weatherman.
- His mother still signs his Christmas gifts as being "From Santa."
- He was Rookie of the Year in 2012.

LEARN SOME MIKE TROUT TRIVIA!

What is Mike's jersey number?

Number 27.

How many World Series wins does Mike Trout have?

As of this writing, none. But he's still one of the greatest players in the league!

Does Mike have a hobby?

He loves to fish!

What's Mike Trout's favorite food?

He loves hamburgers! Especially from his favorite New Jersey restaurant, a joint called Jim's Lunch.

What was his nickname?

The Millville Meteor.

REAL-LIFE LESSONS FROM MIKE TROUT!

- Be ready and be on time.
- Love the game and love yourself.
- Have a good sense of humor.
- Be a team player.
- Have fun.

CONCLUSION
WHAT MADE THEM GREAT?

There are plenty of good players in Major League Baseball. These players are good for a variety of reasons. Some are great batters who can knock the ball out of the park, while others are notoriously gifted pitchers who can strike out batters. These are all great attributes for a Major League player to have, but just being good at hitting or throwing a ball isn't the only thing that makes these guys great. What truly makes a great player is having great character.

Baseball players who truly succeed tend to have great personal qualities related to how they interact with others and their own overall approach in life. They are usually good team players and natural-born problem solvers. This is true whether they are trying to solve their own problems or someone else's. Just take a look at the story of Pedro Martinez and David Ortiz.

Pedro was already a known veteran of the Boston Red Sox when he met David. At the time, David was struggling both on and off the field. His mother had just died, and his future in the big leagues was uncertain, yet Pedro didn't hesitate to extend a helping hand. Thanks to him, David not only stayed in Major League Baseball, but he helped the Boston Red Sox win the World Series after an 86-year drought!

Along with helping David during his time of need, Pedro Martinez also has his own foundation dedicated to giving back to the community. Other big-name baseball players such as Mariano

Rivera, Derek Jeter, and Mark McGwire have also given back considerably through their own charitable organizations.

It's this ability to reach out and do some good that truly makes these guys great. Let that be a lesson to us all—do good, be good, and good things will inevitably follow!

BONUS SECTION:

Positive Affirmations to Help Young Athletes Improve Confidence and Their Mental Game

1. I do a good job
2. I have a lot of energy.
3. I'm successful in what I do.
4. I have confidence.
5. I have good intentions.
6. I'm cooperative.
7. I enjoy being on a team.
8. I will finish well.
9. I will be grateful
10. I respect myself.
11. I am considerate of others.
12. I will utilize my own inner strength.
13. I will dedicate myself to what I do.
14. I practice resilience.
15. I will gain the trust of others.
16. I will stick to the schedule.
17. Creativity will be made use of.
18. I will do my best.
19. I will use my time wisely.
20. I won't be too hard on myself.
21. I am in control of my future.
22. I have pride in what I do.
23. Enjoyment will come easily.
24. I am appreciated.
25. My mind is open to new possibilities.
26. Fulfillment will be obtained.
27. I am special.
28. I am honest and trustworthy.

29. The finish line is within reach.
30. I will keep balanced.
31. Opportunity will come.
32. I will make the most of things.
33. I will get along with others.
34. I will work as a team.
35. I will reach my potential
36. My future looks bright
37. I will keep positivity in focus.
38. I will live and let live.
39. I'll be good to others.
40. I am intelligent and wise.
41. I am patient.
42. I can help others.
43. I am disciplined.
44. I am healthy.
45. I am whole.
46. I can succeed in challenging situations.
47. I can stand on my own two feet.
48. My reward will be great.
49. Honesty is my policy.
50. My mind is focused.
51. I have good instincts.
52. I am patient.
53. I am polite.
54. I will keep in shape.
55. Everything looks good.
56. My team loves me.
57. I'll rack up the points.
58. I will keep going.
59. I'll take things as they come.
60. I will see the value in those around me.
61. I will make plenty of friends.
62. I will help others when I can.

63. I'm on task.

64. I won't have any doubt.

65. I'll keep up with my teammates.

66. I will remain an optimist.

67. I will keep a friendly disposition.

68. I will exercise time management.

69. I will learn many exciting things.

70. I'll train hard.

71. I can pitch and catch with ease.

72. Today's going to be a good day.

73. Each game is fun and exciting.

74. I'm clear headed.

75. I'm not perfect but I will try my best.

76. I will maintain my focus.

77. I play well with others.

78. I am happy.

79. I will take a break when necessary.

80. I won't get upset.

81. I will eat well.

82. I will exercise.

83. I will get enough sleep.

84. I will take a deep breath.

85. I will enjoy myself.

86. I will keep everything in perspective

87. I won't sweat the small things.

88. I will take responsibility for my actions.

89. I'll take it one day at a time.

90. My life sits on a solid foundation.

91. I love myself and others.

92. I accept who I am.

93. I'm eager to take on new challenges.

94. I will make good decisions.

95. Plenty of pleasant things are in store.

96. I enjoy my own company.

97. I will be responsible.
98. Life is a learning experience.
99. I'm an expert at what I do.
100. I have what it takes.
101. I'm equipped to succeed.
102. I'm very talented.
103. My teammates need me.
104. I will see this through to the finish.
105. I'm improving all the time.
106. I have a wide variety of skills.
107. I love to play ball.
108. Life is fun.
109. I'm passionate about baseball.
110. Game day is going to be great!
111. Baseball is my life!
112. I have finely honed concentration.
113. I'm good enough.
114. Life is an incredible journey.
115. I'm in the groove.
116. I have a long time to learn.
117. There's nothing else I'd rather do than play ball.
118. We're on the same team.
119. I can do it.
120. This is going to be great.
121. We're in this together.
122. We can do it.
123. This is wonderful.
124. Being part of a team is awesome.
125. My teammates are my friends.
126. I'm happy when others do well.
127. There's room for all of us to grow.
128. I will play by the rules.
129. I will be kind and good mannered.
130. I will do good.

131.   I will encourage others.
132.   I am bold.
133.   I am satisfied with my life.
134.   I have many unique things to offer.
135.   I am valuable and have self-worth.
136.   I have the support of my teammates.
137.   I have peace.
138.   I'm destined for success.
139.   I release worry and replace it with hope.
140.   Everything I need—I already have.
141.   Quiet time resets and reinvigorates me.
142.   My intuition is my guide.
143.   My path is a positive one.
144.   I think before I speak.
145.   I can overcome any obstacle.
146.   Practice makes me better.
147.   I'm considerate of the feelings of others.
148.   I replace the negative with the positive.
149.   I approve of my own condition.
150.   I give kindness freely as a gift.
151.   I have integrity.
152.   I am trustworthy.
153.   Me and my teammates matter.
154.   I have a unique niche in life.
155.   I will fulfill my purpose.
156.   Life is beautiful.
157.   I am amazed by my own potential.
158.   I inspire others.
159.   I inhale calm and exhale any anxiety.
160.   Everything works out for the best.
161.   I see life with awe and wonder.
162.   Empathy soothes frustration.
163.   Feedback is welcome and refreshing.
164.   I use love to calm conflict.

165.   The past does not control my future.
166.   My heart is in sync with the universe.
167.   All is well.
168.   I am dedicated to the cause.
169.   My teammates will see me at my best.
170.   I will have help along the way.
171.   We are in this together.
172.   I am an eternal optimist.
173.   Everything will turn out well.
174.   I wish everyone the best.
175.   I am happy with myself.
176.   I enjoy trying new things.
177.   I love meeting new people.
178.   My peace is always with me.
179.   I am not dismayed.
180.   Me and my teammates will win.
181.   It's going to be a great game.
182.   I will give voice to my own views.
183.   I am willing to compromise.
184.   I can see things from multiple sides.
185.   There is always room to grow.
186.   Life is rich and expansive.
187.   The future is ours to write.
188.   I have the courage to continue.
189.   I am tenacious.
190.   I can adapt if necessary.
191.   I will live in the present.
192.   I can aid others.
193.   My faith will get me through.
194.   My self-control is rock solid.
195.   Life has many choices to make.
196.   There's never a dull moment.
197.   We're all improving as we go.
198.   My pitches are super-fast!

199. I will catch every ball thrown my way.
200. I will run faster than ever.
201. I will make it to home plate.
202. I will knock the ball out of the park.
203. I won't strike out!
204. I'm a giant on the field.
205. I am all I need to be.
206. I can take things as they come.
207. I listen to my elders.
208. I follow instructions.
209. I'm ready to go.
210. I love to work hard.
211. I will maintain my objectives.
212. I am ready and willing to cooperate.
213. My baseball mitt is ready.
214. There are plenty of good days ahead.
215. Baseball is my favorite sport.
216. I'm happy.
217. I'm learning all the time.
218. I follow the rules.
219. I will be creative.
220. I'll stop and take a breath.
221. I will count my blessings.
222. Baseball is what I do.
223. I'm a problem solver.
224. I believe in healthy competition.
225. My skills are improving.
226. I'm well rested.
227. I am energetic.
228. I have a great gameplan.
229. Me and my teammates will succeed.
230. Victory is within sight.
231. Where there is a will there is a way.
232. I will follow my Heart.

233.   I will keep my close friends close.
234.   I have high endurance.
235.   I am unshakeable.
236.   I will keep going.
237.   I will do it gladly.
238.   I will cooperate.
239.   I'll put my skills to the test.
240.   I enjoy a good challenge.
241.   I will demonstrate success to others.
242.   I have what it takes.
243.   We will get through it together.
244.   I'm getting closer to my goals.
245.   I have the right mentality.
246.   I am helpful.
247.   My example speaks for itself.
248.   I play on a team.
249.   I see the glass half full.
250.   I will play ball.
251.   My bat will connect.
252.   I will run all of the bases.
253.   I will play my position well.
254.   Coach will be impressed.
255.   My teammates will be happy.
256.   I will have the best throwing arm.
257.   My mitt's a magnet for baseballs.
258.   Everything is going to be great.
259.   This will be the best season ever.
260.   My inner light will shine.
261.   I will not be discouraged.
262.   I will not be dismayed.
263.   I will hold my head up high.
264.   I will be all that I can be.
265.   There is no stopping me now.
266.   I will rise in high spirits.

267.   I will go to sleep secure.
268.   My life is on track.
269.   Everything is as it should be.
270.   My team is going to win.
271.   We will go far.
272.   I'm full of potential.
273.   I know how to get things done.
274.   I am well trained.
275.   There is nothing to worry about.
276.   Life is precious.
277.   The bases are loaded.
278.   I am successful.
279.   I have a gift.
280.   I always catch the ball.
281.   Baseball is best.
282.   I have a good grasp of the bat.
283.   My teammates value me.
284.   We will have fun.
285.   Every day is a good day.
286.   I have no fear.
287.   The possibilities are limitless.
288.   I will play like I'm in the Big Leagues.
289.   I'll keep my chin up.
290.   My success is guaranteed.
291.   My mind is focused and alert.
292.   My path is clear.
293.   Every hit and catch counts.
294.   I'm already a pro.
295.   I'll hit plenty of homeruns.
296.   Victory is mine.
297.   I'll never get struck out.
298.   It's full steam ahead.
299.   There's no stopping my team.
300.   We are champs.

301.	Our skills are evident.
302.	I will make everyone proud.
303.	I'm calm and centered.
304.	Baseball is like second nature.
305.	My game is great.
306.	No challenge is too difficult.
307.	I've got all of my bases covered.
308.	The best is yet to come.
309.	I'm the captain of this ship.
310.	I've got full command.
311.	I'm a great baseball player.
312.	I'm in tune with my team.
313.	I have the best coach.
314.	Everyone is doing their part.
315.	We will win.
316.	This is going to be wonderful.
317.	I'm going to have a good time.
318.	I'll listen to my elders.
319.	There are plenty of nice things ahead.
320.	Every day is worth living.
321.	I have a great life.
322.	Time is on my side.
323.	There is nothing too difficult.
324.	Everything is as it should be.
325.	I wear my uniform with pride.
326.	I can't wait to play ball.
327.	There are plenty of things to learn.
328.	I have everything I want.
329.	I am completely satisfied.
330.	Nothing is lacking.
331.	I have good feelings for all.
332.	There is nothing at all amiss.
333.	The Baseball Diamond is my favorite place to be in the whole wide world.

THE MENTAL MINDSET TO HELP YOU SUCCEED IN BASEBALL

Baseball is a competitive sport and eager young players want to succeed. Having such a mindset is crucial in order to do your best in baseball. Even so, you can't always come out a winner. There will indeed be ups and downs in the game of baseball as well as the game of life. We need to develop the right kind of mindset so that we can handle any challenge we may face.

AFFIRMATION

To get started on the path of success, you first need to believe in your own abilities. That's why we use affirmations to boost our confidence and sense of self-worth. Affirmations do not have to be repeated on a daily basis, but they should be reflected upon from time to time. You could even simply write them down on bits of paper or some other surface you might routinely take notice of. However you do it, just make sure to keep these positive and encouraging words front and center in your mind.

FACE YOUR EMOTIONS

Emotions are a part of life. How we handle them means everything. Emotions can express our joy or even help us to vent some frustration. But too much emotion can also hinder our progress. That's why it's important to learn how to get a good handle on how to deal with our emotions. We shouldn't ignore our feelings, but we should not be overwhelmed by them either. We should be able to take them at face value, and then logically sort through any feelings that we may have.

SET GOALS

In order to keep your mind focused, we need to set goals for ourselves. Goals help us see our progress in real time as we achieve greater and even more impressive objectives. Nothing boosts the confidence more than a job well done.

BE A TEAM PLAYER

Baseball is a team effort. You need to develop the mindset of being a team player. Crucial in this development is learning to work with others. If you've never played on a team, you can start by simply learning to cooperate with family members. Families after all, are the first team we are a part of—*we're born into them!* Knowing how to cooperate with your family is a great foundation to already have in place when you join a baseball team. You can then think of the baseball team as an even larger family, with a much more diverse cast of characters to learn to cooperate with.

ACKNOWLEDGE THERE IS ALWAYS MORE TO LEARN

Life is a learning process, and the sooner we acknowledge that we are still learning, the better our mindset will be. Don't approach anything in life as if you are an absolute expert. Keep an open mind and be willing to learn new things. Being willing to learn is what allows one to improve. This means being willing to take criticism and learn from previous mistakes.

THE TEAMS

Baseball teams play in what is termed a "baseball diamond." The core of the baseball diamond is the four bases that make up it's diamond shape. Circling the field in a counterclockwise direction, we have first base, second base, third base, and home plate. The team which is at bat, are the one's who have their batter stand at home plate. The batter hits the ball and runs from home plate to first base, with the intention of running all the way back to home. Further out from the bases is what's called the "outfield." The team which is not at bat, has players in the outfield ready to catch the batter's ball in order to give him an "out." They also throw the ball to their players standing at the bases, to shortstop, as well as back to their pitcher who is positioned in the middle of the field, directly across from home plate on the pitcher's mound. The teams switch places after three outs.

EQUIPMENT

Basic baseball gear consists of the players uniforms, cleats, baseball gloves, bats, and of course baseballs. Batter's typically also wear protective batting helmets in order to protect them from oncoming baseballs.

PLAYING BASICS

Baseball games consist of nine innings. During each of these innings, one team is at bat while the other team is in the field. The batter stands at homebase with the intention to hit the ball pitched by the other team. The other team's pitcher throws the ball. The ball may be thrown straight to the pitcher in what is called the "strike zone" or it might curve to the left or right. Batter's do not have to swing at curve balls. If the ball is out of the strike zone, the batter can simply let the ball pass. This is called taking a "ball." The batter can take up to four balls, and after that they are allowed to walk to base. If the ball is thrown well within the strike zone, the batter will swing and try and hit it. If the batter misses, then the missed swing is called a "strike." If the batter gets three strikes, they are called out. If the batter hits the ball, they can run to base. Once a team gets three outs, the roles alternate and the other team is at bat.

RULES TO KEEP IN MIND

Baseball is a fun sport, but it's also a sport of rules. In order to be successful we have to have a good understanding of what those rules are.

Some specific rules to keep in mind are:

- Three strikes you're out.
- Four balls and you walk.
- Balls hit out of bounds are foul balls and do not count.
- Three outs end an inning.

www.ingramcontent.com/pod-product-compliance
Lightning Source LLC
Chambersburg PA
CBHW050742150726
48196CB00003B/320